THE FOUR CORNERSTONES OF FINANCIAL WELLBEING

CREATE A PATHWAY TO A MORE HEALTHY AND MEANINGFUL LIFE

CHRIS BUDD

Published by
LID Publishing
An imprint of LID Business Media Ltd.
LABS House, 15-19 Bloomsbury Way,
London, WC1A 2TH, UK

info@lidpublishing.com
www.lidpublishing.com

A member of:

businesspublishersroundtable.com

Printed by Severn, Gloucester
ISBN: 978-1-911687-76-4
ISBN: 978-1-911687-77-1 (ebook)

Cover and page design: Caroline Li

THE FOUR CORNERSTONES OF FINANCIAL WELLBEING

CREATE A PATHWAY TO A MORE HEALTHY AND MEANINGFUL LIFE

CHRIS BUDD

MADRID | MEXICO CITY | LONDON
BUENOS AIRES | BOGOTA | SHANGHAI

CONTENTS

INTRODUCTION

Money is a means of exchange. Centuries ago, under the barter system, ten chickens may have been exchanged for one sheep or a wheel repair. This did, however, involve taking a lot of chickens around with you. Money allowed one sheep to be sold for one unit, which could then be exchanged for ten chickens or the wheel repair. The function of money was to make transactions easier.

Money does, of course, continue to fulfil this function. One unit of money still equals one sheep. At some point, however, money also started buying other things, such as status. One person only needs a certain number of sheep. But the appetite for status is insatiable.

Our relationship with money has shifted from a transactional one to an accumulation-focused one, where the focus is on accumulating more wealth rather than having 'enough.' Money should serve us, but it has somehow gained control over us and become our master.

It remains a means of exchange, but now money is also exchanged for goods that are purchased not for practical reasons, but to bring prestige. Expensive cars acquired because they are a way of showing others that you can afford to drive an expensive car. Personalised numberplates. Designer clothing, expensive because it is expensive. For many, prestige has become a bigger priority than practicality.

In this process, something has been lost. Many of us search for meaning and joy in our lives, not realising that money has become a barrier to wellbeing.

How has this happened? Answering this is the subject of *Part One* of this book. It shows how our programming, from our ancestors and from modern society, tempts us down one path, whereas there is greater wellbeing to be found in another direction.

Money can also be exchanged for time. This might be time a long way into the future, such as retirement. It might be time now, such as leisure time, or the ability to choose what you do during the working day.

Financial wellbeing is a broad subject area that looks at the relationship between money and happiness. *Part Two* of this book sheds light on our relationship with money, and how it can be changed in order to live a happier life. Money is an engine for wellbeing, but it can also be an engine for misery.

Which route you choose to go down is in your own hands.

MY FINANCIAL
WELLBEING JOURNEY

When I came up with the title for what would be *The Financial Wellbeing Book* in 2015, I googled the term 'financial wellbeing' to make sure the title had not been used before.[1] There were *two* results in that search.

I've just googled the term again. Now there are *256 million* results!

That original book gave a practical pathway for how to create a financial plan for your money that is designed to make you happier as well as wealthier. As such, it was focused on using money to generate wellbeing.

In the intervening years, I have written more than 90 episodes of *The Financial Wellbeing Podcast* and founded the Institute for Financial Wellbeing. I have learned so much more about the relationship between money and happiness in that time. I've come to understand the impact of money on our health, and how having a better relationship with money will reduce stress levels.

The Financial Wellbeing Book guided the reader to create a financial plan to become happier, not just wealthier. *The Four Cornerstones of Financial Wellbeing* now digs deeper into our relationship with money in order to examine why we make poor financial decisions and to enable you to create your own wellbeing plan. This will lead to a healthier relationship with money, leading to a more joyful life.

This book is based on the research of many people (all of whom I have referenced). There are also ideas of my own, based on my many years of advising clients, as a financial planner and as a coach.

I believe that we could all be happier – both individually and as a society – if we revised our relationship with money. The book is aimed at individuals, but this principle extends to companies (purpose over profit, and more collaboration with less competition) and to governments (policies designed to increase wellbeing, not wealth).

Let us consider what we might do to help ourselves to be *happier and healthier*, not just wealthier.

HOW THE BOOK WORKS

The book is structured into two parts.

Part One provides insight into the extent of the challenge that we face in changing our relationship to money. It looks at how we are not programmed to create a financial plan that is focused on our happiness. It also examines why the stakes are so high, due to the impact on our health as well as our wealth.

In *Part Two* we look at the research on happiness and apply this to money, enabling you to create your own financial wellbeing plan.

The appendices are an important part of this book. *Appendix 1: Your Financial Wellbeing Plan*, in particular, brings together the various activities that will help you create your own financial wellbeing plan.

TIP FOR FINANCIAL ADVISERS: You will find these boxes dotted throughout the book. They are tips for financial advisers who want to bring focus to the way in which they deliver their financial planning and financial advice to their clients. If this is you, then you may wish to read *Appendix 4, A Note For Financial Advisers* before reading on.

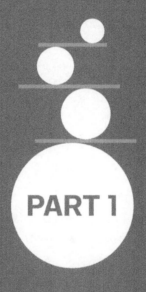

PART 1

WHY WE NEED A NEW APPROACH TO MONEY

CHAPTER 1

● ● ● ●

THE
CHALLENGE

This book provides tools to enable you to create a financial wellbeing plan – a plan for life that is designed to make you happier and healthier, not just wealthier.

In creating such a plan, we should first address the nature of the challenge that we face. How does our current attitude towards money (both individually and as a society) contribute to – or work against – our wellbeing? Is this something we can change, or is it built into how we make financial decisions?

In *Part One*, therefore, we will look at how our relationship with money often works against our own wellbeing. We will look back over the history of humankind to discover the many reasons which suggest that we are simply not hardwired to be good with money, especially when planning for the long term. Finally, we will look at how our broken relationship with money affects us physically as well as mentally.

SUMMARISING THE PROBLEM

Let me start by summarising the central premise of this book, which explains why we are not capable of making good, long-term financial decisions.[2]

There are three factors that must be present in order for us to want to get out of bed and do things. To be motivated. They are:
- Competence (we are able to do the thing)
- Relatedness (the thing connects us with others, including our future selves)
- Autonomy (the thing allows us to control our destiny and behaviours)

We will be looking at this theory in greater detail in *Chapter 7*. It is important not to think of these three factors as either *present* or *not present* when we make financial decisions. Rather, the more we have of each of the factors, the greater our motivation. The trouble is that, when it comes to thinking long term about money, these elements are, at best, limited.

We have limited **competence** with money because:
- Prior to the Industrial Revolution we rarely needed to plan beyond the next season
- We have not needed to put money aside for a post-work period until the last 40 years of human history
- We are not taught about money (and, if we are, the education focuses on budgeting and facts)
- We make financial decisions on the basis of a fight-or-flight response

We get limited **relatedness** from money because:
- Financial planning is for the benefit of our future selves, which feels like giving money away to someone else
- Connecting with others comes from having meaning and purpose, whereas our economic system relies on competition
- As a result we tend to associate money with consumption and accumulation, not connecting with others

We get limited **autonomy** from money because:
- We tend to see success in terms of external rewards such as status, power, fame and money
- Because these rewards are given by others, we need to keep chasing them
- More money does not therefore give more control, yet this seductive belief continues

Because we do not have these three factors in place, we tend to have a poor relationship with money – one where we see money as an objective, rather than as an engine for wellbeing. We spend today rather than plan for the future.

SUMMARISING THE SOLUTION

This book will identify ways in which we can overcome each of these issues, meaning that we make better financial decisions and therefore have better financial outcomes.

We can increase our **competence** with money by:
- Accepting that good financial decisions require positive action to overcome our natural instincts
- Educating ourselves about the relationship between money and wellbeing
- Understanding what leads us to make instinctive decisions about money: our behavioural biases and self-limiting beliefs

We can increase our **relatedness** from money by:
- Taking steps to better connect with our future selves
- Focusing on the real sources of joy
- And thereby increasing our connections with others

We can increase our **autonomy** from money by:
- Understanding that it is internal rewards that bring joy to our lives (connecting with others, and having meaning and purpose)
- Working out how much is enough to do those things that bring us joy
- And thereby regain control of our future because money is no longer the destination, but just one of the ways to get us there

In this way, you will better understand the role of money in serving you, rather than controlling you, which will lead you to make better financial decisions and have a healthier relationship with money. You can use your money to accumulate experiences and create a fulfilling life, rather than spending your life accumulating wealth.

With the premise of this book outlined, let's look at a few underlying principles that will help us to find a better relationship with money.

IT'S NOT YOUR FAULT

Many of our assumptions about what makes us happy – and in particular how money makes us happy – are misguided. There are lots of reasons why our relationship with money has developed in this way. The good news is that if you feel you are not very good with money, it's not your fault. Indeed, not only are you not alone – you are actually in the majority!

> In my twenties, I smoked cigarettes. Around the time I decided to give up, I saw an advert about quitting smoking featuring John Cleese.
>
> One fact made all the difference to me. Mr Cleese stated that the addictive element of cigarettes stays in your body for 14 days.[3] If you felt a craving during that time, the message went, it wasn't that you were in some way being 'weak' – it was the chemical at work.
>
> This helped me to understand that there were outside forces at work and that my addiction was not my 'fault.' This gave me great hope, as I now had something to combat; it helped me realise that I was in control of the process.

We will spend time understanding the forces at work in the modern relationship between money and happiness in order to plot our way to a financial wellbeing plan. The aim is to be better with money. A good starting point, then, is to ask: What does 'better with money' actually mean? How will we know when we have achieved being 'better with money'? What is our destination?

MAKE HAPPINESS THE OBJECTIVE

The Chinese philosopher Lao Tzu once said: "The journey of a thousand miles begins with one step."[4]

But in which direction?

Sometimes we can get so tangled up trying to get the perfect plan in place, we forget to take sufficient time to think about the destination.

This is a particular problem when it comes to dealing with money. All too often, financial plans aim to make us wealthier, to help us achieve financial goals or enable purchases. They rarely have happiness as their objective.

This is because Western society is built on the notion that financial success will make us happy. We are surrounded by images of wealth and status as being some kind of utopia. And yet the newspapers are full of wealthy people who are unhappy, and lottery winners who end up getting divorced or giving their winnings away.

If financial success is not making us happy, then is it really success?

Maybe the definitions of success that we are given in Western culture are actually misleading.

> Books with titles such as *How to Get Rich* or *The Hab-its of the Rich and Famous* are all trying to sell you a dream that being rich is great and that only they have the secret. In fact, there really is a secret. How do you get rich quick? Just write a book called *How to Get Rich Quick*!
>
> The trouble with these types of books is that they start from the premise that being rich is the objective. But 'being rich' does not automatically mean you will be happy. The very premise of such books is flawed.

When we say 'better with money', therefore, we mean using our money to accumulate life, not the other way around – creating a financial wellbeing plan that will move our focus away from accumulating wealth and on to living a joyful life. Let's start our quest to understand financial wellbeing by defining it not in terms of wealth or status but in terms of happiness. Let us define our own success, not let others define it for us.

THE DANGER IN SEARCHING FOR HAPPINESS
In searching for the sources of happiness and their relationship with money, there is another trap into which we must be careful not to fall.

Our objective is to create a financial wellbeing plan that will send our future selves the gift of happiness – to learn what we might do *now* in order to bestow that gift.

In order to be happier, we might read lots of books about how to be happy. Like this one! But this can mean spending so much time thinking about *how* to be happy, we forget to actually *be* happy. A bit like trying to dig your way out of a hole. Or the person standing among some trees complaining they are stopping them from being able to see the wood.

"Obsessing about getting what you want and avoiding what you don't want does not result in happiness."[5]

We need to think carefully about our desired destination – and to be careful that we are not simply headed round in circles. "The very attempt to seek happiness can become endless, and trying to get rid of our stress can just make more of it."[6]

There are many distractions in our lives that nudge us in the wrong direction. Societal pressure to be rich and beautiful, to have status and to influence others, and so on.

As a consequence of all this noise, we end up either not doing anything now or heading off in a direction that doesn't lead to happiness. As a result, our future self does not become as happy as they might be.

Research shows that this is more difficult for people in economic hardship – worries about money stop us from thinking about what will bring us joy and purpose.[7] Just because something is difficult, however, doesn't mean it shouldn't be done. This isn't about being right or wrong, being happy or not happy; it is about making incremental improvements that will last.

Indeed, the very fact that happiness is not permanent can mean that being happy actually makes us unhappy, as we know it will not last! There is even a name for this – cherophobia, an aversion to or fear of being happy.

Instead, therefore, we should be seeking a more permanent type of happiness. For the purpose of this book, we will use the idea that *happiness* is temporary but *wellbeing* is longer lasting.

THREE STEPS TO ACHIEVING FINANCIAL WELLBEING

I would suggest that there are three steps to creating a financial wellbeing plan.

First, we need to start with Step Two.

Starting at the beginning is not always the right answer. By focusing on the beginning, we risk being unable to clearly see the destination. Unable to see the point, we don't bother to start at all. Let's therefore start by looking at Step Two:

Step Two: Understand that happiness comes from within

If we obtain our joy, our self-worth, from external sources – perhaps fame, possessions, status – then we find ourselves on a treadmill of trying to please other people. We might succeed in achieving happiness; however, it will be temporary, only there as long as others bestow it upon us. We can become stressed and worn out trying to please others.

If, however, we find our joy, our self-worth, from within, from living a life with meaning and purpose, then this will provide much deeper and more satisfying wellbeing. This also happens to be good for our bodies – a healthier way of living.

Which leads to the question: if we get external self-worth from others, how do we develop self-worth from within? The answer to this forms Step Three:

Step Three: Be compassionate

A wonderful expression of this principle comes from what the Dalai Lama calls having a "warm heart."[8] Compassion, a focus on helping and being kind to others, will develop our internal joy and sense of self-worth.

What might be stopping us from getting to Steps Two and Three? One reason is that we are taught from a young age to strive, to work hard, to achieve, to aim for financial rewards. Images of success invariably involve wealth or possessions. Pathways to success are always upwards, and achievement is depicted as standing at the top. Success is always somewhere different, and it invariably happens to someone else.

As a result of this emphasis on material possessions as signifying success, we don't have the space in our heads to actively develop our internal self-worth.

In my career in financial planning, I've noticed that when a person reaches financial security, the most common next step is to consider how they can help others. They 'send the lift back down.' Options include charity roles, mentoring, coaching, philanthropy and investing in start-up businesses.

Which begs the question: why have they not made this a focus of their lives before? The answer is because they have been too busy trying to achieve financial security. They have been unable to see the destination.

Now that we can see the destination, we can come back around to Step One:

Step One: Create a financial wellbeing plan for a happy future

There is something blocking our view to Steps Two and Three. And that thing is money, and the idea that financial independence comes from accumulation of wealth. If we become more aware of what makes us happy, we will find that financial independence moves nearer to where we currently are.

We need to be able to look past Step One, the financial plan, to see what is in store in Steps Two and Three. We need to see the destination. Only then will we have the inspiration to embark on Step One.

This means that we need to:

put some thought into our own individual definitions for success

Which requires us to:

understand the factors that work against a healthy relationship with money

In addition, we're going to need to:

understand what brings happiness, and what brings wellbeing

It would also be helpful if we could:

identify the distractions and barriers that stop us from achieving wellbeing

Only then are we likely to change our focus from external to internal self-worth. With this insight we can create a financial wellbeing plan that is unique to each of us.

CONCLUSION

If we are going to create better financial outcomes – by which I mean financial outcomes which increase or at least maintain our wellbeing – then we must first acknowledge that this is something we need to work at. In *Chapter 3* we will look at the historical reasons why we find creating a financial plan so difficult. First, though, let's think a bit more deeply about where we are headed, and how will we recognise when we have arrived.

● ● ● ●

CHAPTER 2

WHAT IS YOUR DEFINITION OF SUCCESS?

We have established the importance of knowing the destination before setting off in the right direction. Before we get into happiness theory, therefore, we should spend some time looking at where we are planning to go. We need to think about what success will look like.

We might think that this should be fairly easy. In fact, what we think of as success is influenced by many factors, and not all of them are helpful.

THE TRAPPINGS OF SUCCESS

The Western world tends to define success in financial terms.

Only if someone sells their business for lots of money are they typically deemed to be a successful businessperson. A person who runs a business that employs people who are fulfilled and that produces products or services that bring joy to their clients, but that makes only a small profit, would not typically be considered a successful entrepreneur.

A football manager who wins the Champions League and is appointed national team coach on a huge salary would be considered a success. The coach for a village under 9s team who teaches children the basic skills and brings the community together is unlikely to be lauded as a success. Or appreciated. Or possibly even noticed.

> The film *Slumdog Millionaire* won the Oscar for Best Picture in 2009. You might know that its star was Dev Patel. You may know that it was directed by Danny Boyle. But you probably don't know that it was written by Simon Beaufoy.
>
> You're probably even less likely to know that it was based on a novel called *Q & A* by Vikas Swarup. Boyle and Beaufoy both won Oscars (alongside the seven other Oscars the film won). There is, however, no Oscar category for 'best original idea from which a film was made.'

The way that we value things is equally skewed. A nurse might earn 100 times less than the private equity financier they are saving the life of. Each year, during the Budget speech, the Chancellor announces the plans for the government to increase the Gross Domestic Product of the country, but says nothing about our wellbeing. A tree has no economic value until it is cut down and turned into furniture.[9]

When we live in a society where this hierarchy of reward is the norm, when the priorities of society are so misaligned with wellbeing, it is hardly surprising that we struggle to prioritise and understand what makes us happy.

KNOWING SUCCESS WHEN YOU SEE IT

What *is* success? What will it look like? You work hard, you work smart, you compete and you innovate. At what point in time do you sit back, relax and think "I've made it"? Will this be on the back of a yacht (perhaps with a big cigar), or maybe just in an easy chair in the conservatory? The key question is *what will be your destination?*

How will you *know* when you are successful?

IMAGES OF SUCCESS

Can you even be sure that your image of success is, indeed, yours? Consider what TV and the media portray as being successful. The images that we are presented with are what create our expectations of success. What do they suggest success looks like?

Take the TV programme *Dragon's Den*, for example. Here are five successful entrepreneurs, each with a big wad of money on the table in front of them. That's a pretty clear image! These rich people have the power to change the lives of those budding entrepreneurs if they choose to invest in their dreams. Those dragons have *power* and they have *money*.

Then there are programmes like *The X Factor*. They are about making money from art, turning creativity into a competition. For the victor, there is a contract that can lead to *fame* and *influence* and, of course, riches. The joy from creativity and performance is sold for money.

Endless television programmes show how you can make money from property. This changes the definition of homes to investment.

The media portrays being successful in terms of *power, influence, money and fame.*

Where does happiness fit in?

> Mark McCormack pretty much invented the business of sport, back in the 1960s. He became agent to golfer Arnold Palmer when there was no such thing as a sporting agent. His company, IMG, is now a huge worldwide management agency in the world of sports people and celebrities.
>
> McCormack wrote a wonderful book called *What They Don't Teach You at Harvard Business School*.[10] It is full of anecdotes and tips. My father gave me a copy of the book when I was 17. It's a great read. All the stories slowly build up into one unifying message offering McCormack's secret to success:
>
> **In order to succeed in business, be nice to people.**

It would be churlish to suggest that money doesn't bring happiness or that it should not feature in a definition of success. Richard Gere once said, "Having lots of money doesn't make you happy, but it does mean you can drive through the French countryside during a weekday."[11]

There are other definitions of success than money, however. Personally, I define success by the positive impact that I have, and having flexibility in the use of my time. The great thing about this definition is that if I get it right, happiness follows.

YOUR DEFINITION OF SUCCESS

One of the slogans I have been using for many years about financial planning is this:

Financial planning is really very simple; you simply work out what you want from life then spend your money on that.

The trouble is, working out what you want from life isn't so easy. Even when you think you have it nailed, you often realise that you have built your ideal life on wobbly assumptions.

A friend told me over lunch that she was planning to take a year out, which she would spend with her husband on a remote Scandinavian island. She had built up a marketing consultancy over the previous decade, and now wanted to take a break.

I asked her what she was going to do during the year, in between growing and rearing their own food. She replied that she had so many innovative ideas about marketing but had never had the time to write them down because she had been so busy. She therefore planned on using the year to finally write that book about marketing.

Rather carefully, I suggested that she seemed to be planning to spend her entire year away from marketing doing nothing but... thinking about marketing!

We will look at finding what brings *you* wellbeing in greater detail in *Part Two*, which might be summarised as the 'know thyself' part of this book. It would be useful, however, to have an idea of the destination in mind from the outset. To get your financial wellbeing plan started, you may wish to undertake Exercise 1 in *Appendix 1: Your Financial Wellbeing Plan*, relating to your definition of success.

Once you have completed this exercise, you should be in a better position to write down your own definition of success. Don't work too hard on it and don't worry if you haven't got it quite right. It will almost certainly change or be modified as we go through the principles of financial wellbeing. At this point, just make sure it feels like *your* definition.

THE COMFORT IN KNOWING YOUR PLAN WILL BE WRONG

As German Field Marshal Helmuth von Moltke (1800–91) said, "No plan of operations reaches with any certainty beyond the first encounter with the enemy's main force."[12]

Let's dial down the pressure here. Talking about finding happiness, wellbeing or success can seem pretty daunting. We will focus on doing some things that will make things a bit better. Let's acknowledge that some things will work, and others might need revising. The single thing we know with absolute certainty about a plan is that it will change.[13] So let us embrace this fact.

We know that your plan is not going to turn out exactly as you intend. Life has that way of setting you off in one direction, then opening some doors and closing others. What we are trying to build here is something that will get you started, knowing that you are going to look in often to check in and reassess.

CONCLUSION

This plan that we will be building does not need to be perfect or life changing. You don't need to make irreversible decisions. Just try to head off in roughly the right direction, then review, review, review.

Having gained a reasonable grasp of where we are headed, let's take a moment to look at some of the reasons why we find planning for our financial future to be so difficult. Let's see what we are up against as we construct our financial wellbeing plan.

• • • •

MONEY AND STRESS: PROGRAMMED TO BE BAD WITH MONEY

How did the move from money as a means of exchange to money as an objective come about? We will now look at some of the forces that have brought us to this position, in order to unravel and review some of our financial assumptions.

You are not programmed to make good decisions about money. It's not your fault! Decisions about money, and about the future, are difficult and stressful. In this chapter, we will look at why this is.

HOW WE MAKE DECISIONS

We have two ways of making decisions. They are known in psychology as System 1 and System 2, but we might know them better through the shorthand of 'gut decisions' and 'considered decisions.'[14]

Gut decisions tend to be made quickly. Would I like an ice cream? Should I cross the road now? Shall I dance?

Considered decisions require two things: time and information. Would I like to go to see a film on Thursday night? It depends on which film and whether I'm busy. I'll look into it and get back to you.

Let me illustrate this with another example. If we were stood in a field and I asked you which was the quickest way out, you would immediately point to the nearest gate. You wouldn't need much time and the matter wouldn't require much thought. This is System 1.

If, on the other hand, I asked you how long it would take a bull to run 30 metres when the average speed of a typical bull is 35 miles per hour, you might be able to work out the answer, but it would take some time and probably require the aid of a pen, a piece of paper and perhaps a calculator. In other words, it would need to be a more considered answer. This is System 2.

Now, suppose I asked you for the quickest way out of a field when at that very moment there was a bull charging towards us from 30 metres away. It might be a System 1-type decision, but the fact that you would be impaled on the horns of an angry bull in a few seconds' time would make answering the question extremely stressful!

System 1 decision-making is great when the stakes are not too high, when we don't need much time or when we are considering a relatively simple question. These are fight-or-flight decisions and the system goes back many millions of years to when these were the typical decisions that we needed to make each day, when we were prey. This is how our brains are wired, to make these decisions all the time.

If we don't have the information upon which to base an informed decision, then trying to make System 2 decisions will be stressful, and we are likely to use System 1 – a gut decision. If we don't have sufficient time to make a considered decision, then we will have no choice but to revert to using System 1.

Making a System 1 decision about something with a potentially huge impact on your life is going to be stressful.

In many ways, therefore, we could say that financial wellbeing is all about trying to slow down the financial decisions we make, so that we make them with System 2, not System 1. Your financial wellbeing plan therefore needs *time* and it needs *information* – for example about what makes you happy. Which is why this book exists!

FINANCIAL PLANNING DECISIONS ARE LONG-TERM DECISIONS

One of the issues around making a money decision is that it so often has a long-term ramification. If we regularly buy our lunch from a local delicatessen, that is a fairly easy decision, made using System 1. If we stop to think about the cumulative effect on our finances of those regular System 1 decisions, it might become a harder decision to continually justify. We might see the financial sense in batch cooking or in making a sandwich at home the night before. This would involve delaying the enjoyment from our money and creating effort for long-term gain.

We don't tend to favour decisions that delay gratification. It is therefore a consideration that we try to avoid, and continue buying lunch from the delicatessen. When it comes to money, we often avoid using System 2.

And this must surely *always* be an issue when we are creating a financial plan. Because, by definition, the process of financial planning involves looking at the future – a place about which we know very little for certain!

THE HISTORY OF PERSONAL FINANCIAL RESPONSIBILITY

Human activity over the millennia has been driven by the desire to feel safe and secure. It is only in recent times – *very* recent times – that humans have been required to think about such huge long-term concepts as how much money we might need in the future.

The average wage of an Italian peasant in the early 13th century was the equivalent of $1,600. Move forward some six hundred years, and the average wage of an Italian peasant in the 19th century was... $1,600.[15] When you grow and rear your own food, you don't need to worry about a pay rise. Your time frame is the seasons. When you don't live beyond a working age, or if you have a family to look after you if you are no longer able to work, you don't need to think about putting money into a pension fund for your retirement.

Life expectancy in the UK alone increased from 71 years in 1960 to 81 years in 2019.[16] That's an additional ten years of not working for which we now need to save.

THE SHIFT IN RESPONSIBILITY FOR YOUR FUTURE

At the same time that we began to live longer lives, capitalism evolved, and we went from being farmers or tradespeople to being employees. Instead of growing or rearing our own food, we worked for someone else and used the money to buy food. Our lives began to include a period in which we stopped working but still needed an income. Retirement was born!

Large employers began to take responsibility for their employees. One of the earliest private occupational pension schemes was the Chartered Gas Light and Coke Company Superannuation Fund, set up in 1841. Other early occupational schemes included those of

Reuters (1882) and W. H. Smith (1894).[17] These pension schemes required no decisions from the individual employees and had no investments for them to manage – the employer simply continued to pay an income after the person stopped working, to an amount usually dependant on length of service with the company and salary at the time of retirement. Company pension schemes like these became known as 'financial salary schemes,' more recently renamed 'defined benefit pension schemes.'

Governments responded more slowly. State pensions for all started to be provided in Germany in the 1880s. Pensions for municipal workers in the USA began to be provided in the mid-19th century.[18] In the UK, the Old Age Pensions Act was passed in 1908 – although eligibility for this pension relied on being of "good character"![19] The state pension didn't arrive until 1946. In this way, governments and private employers took responsibility for the retirement income of their workers.

Only in 1988, when Margaret Thatcher's government introduced private personal pensions, were employees given the ability to manage their own investments within their pension fund. They were not, however, given any education or training on how to do so – meaning System 2 decisions about your pension were impossible to make.

Then, newspaper owner Robert Maxwell 'fell' off his boat, and his pillaging of the Mirror Group company pension scheme was uncovered. The government brought in swathes of new legislation in order to protect other pension scheme members – with the unintended consequence that the private sector closed almost all of its defined benefit schemes.

These changes, which only arrived over the past 40 years of humankind's long history, have meant that the responsibility for funding our futures has been moved onto the shoulders of us, the individual. However, as someone wise once said, "with great power comes great responsibility"[20] – a responsibility that we are entirely unsuited to handle.

Savings, pensions, investment portfolios, risk diversity – these are not concepts that we are used to. There is no education on such subjects in schools. Yet now, more than ever before, we are required to set money aside for an (ever longer) financial future.

We need to use System 2 to make financial planning decisions, but we have little information and even less education. At the same time, the importance of those decisions has risen almost exponentially. As a result, financial planning has become ever more stressful.

SHORT-TERM GAIN FOR LONG-TERM PAIN

When we make financial decisions, we are purchasing emotional comfort.[21] We want to make ourselves feel better *now*. We will do this even if it means sacrificing happiness later. Worries about money can cloud our judgement when setting priorities.

There are unlikely to be many 20-year-olds who consider the size of their pension fund to be a priority. And equally there are unlikely to be many 60-year-olds who don't. But it is the same person, just 40 years apart.

A patient having treatment for chemotherapy failed to turn up for one of his sessions. When he arrived for the next session four days later, he explained that he was reliant upon income support and had had an appointment at the job centre. He was worried that if he hadn't turned up to that meeting, his income support would have stopped.

He was so concerned to ensure that his rent was paid and that he would have enough money for food and groceries that he prioritised attending the meeting at the job centre over having chemotherapy – literally putting his life at risk.[22]

Part of the reason that we make quick and emotional decisions – System 1 decisions – when it comes to our finances is that it is far easier to make a decision based on information that we know and that is available to us. If the stock market falls dramatically, we can take action now to get out, based on what we see is happening. It may well be that we have seen the stock market fall and rise many times and in our heads we know that the market will come back. But we have no proof of that, and so we take action based upon what we see in front of us.

In March 2020, stock markets around the world plummeted in reaction to the global Covid-19 pandemic. The FTSE 100 went from around 7,500 in mid-February to 4,993 on 23 March, recovering slightly to 5,454 by 1 April.

The abiding rule of investing is 'buy low, sell high,' right? Well, in the month of March 2020, the net retail outflow from UK markets was £9.7 billion, a record by a factor of almost four times the next highest.[23] In other words, as markets fell, investors got out. The FTSE 100 only nudged back over 7,000 in April 2021.

> This is a story repeated during all sudden market move-
> ments, whether it be the outflow from the Nasdaq
> (the American technology market) during the dot-com
> crash of the early 2000s or the global financial crisis
> of 2008. We tend to invest emotionally – we buy high
> and sell low.

One way to overcome this instinct to make decisions based on
the short term is to set up rules and processes that you cannot
override. For example, set up a regular payment into a savings
account. For more on this, see Exercise 2 in *Appendix 1: Your
Financial Wellbeing Plan.*

CONNECTING WITH
YOUR FUTURE SELF

Savings, pensions, life assurance – these all involve trying to
guess what might happen in the future. But herein lies a fundamental problem: we find it very difficult to think about ourselves
in the future.

Studies by neuroscientists have shown that we tend to use one
part of our brain when we think about ourselves and a different
part when we think about other people.[24] When we try to picture
ourselves in the future, we use the part of our brain that *thinks about
someone else.*

The further away the future self that you are trying to imagine, the
worse your brain gets at recognising you. As a consequence, we are
not always motivated to help our future self, as this feels like we
are giving money to someone else.

Connecting with your future self could be the change that has the biggest impact on your spending and saving habits. If you can connect better with your future self, you may also find yourself saving more.

There are some suggestions about how to connect with your future self in Exercise 3 in *Appendix 1: Your Financial Wellbeing Plan*. These rest on two key principles. First, you need to recognise yourself. For example, some product providers have used ageing software to show you what you will look like in the future. Care is needed here, however – if you find it upsetting to see yourself in the future, then this is unlikely to be motivating!

Second, there is the fact that our future is far from certain. The person you are today is different from the person you were a year ago – and is also different from the person you will be in a year's time. There is research that suggests that we acknowledge the changes that have happened to us in the past while simultaneously rejecting the likelihood of such changes happening in the future.[25]

Your ability to connect with your future self will be stronger if you have a clear mental image of yourself in the future. This will then have an impact on your behaviours now.[26] However, this does not need to solely derive from picturing yourself or your circumstances physically; you also need to understand yourself on an emotional level that acknowledges your sense of purpose. It may be helpful to imagine having the time to be creative, to run the café you've always dreamed of or to volunteer in a charity to help others. However, it may be less useful to imagine a fantasy house that you've dreamed of living in.

It is also important to be able to see how you might get there – to have a clear path to identifiable objectives (we'll be looking at the word 'objectives' in much greater detail in *Chapter 8*).

Your ability to connect with your future self relies on you being able to see how your objectives might be achieved. One way of doing this is cashflow forecasting – for example, by using a qualified financial planner.

TIP FOR FINANCIAL ADVISERS: Look at Exercise 3, about connecting with your future self, in *Appendix 1: Your Financial Wellbeing Plan.* Your clients' output from this exercise should be a costed look at how they want to live in the future. Could you use this in your cashflow reporting to create the 'clear path' that is important in identifying a clearer picture of the future self, and thereby improving financial wellbeing?

CONCLUSION

We can see that, when it comes to money and thinking about our futures, we do not have the history, training, knowledge or instincts to make good decisions. We make financial decisions with System 1 when they need to be made with System 2. This means that money decisions are fearful and stressful.

Before we move on to look at what we can do about this, let's take a look to see how this might be affecting our health.

CHAPTER 4

●●●●

WHY WEALTH CAN BE BAD FOR YOUR HEALTH

In order to put money back into its proper place, we need to not spend so much time thinking about it. Indeed, it could be argued that the central premise of any book about financial wellbeing should be to not read books about money! According to research by Aegon, more than half (55%) of average earners and more than one in three of society's top earners worry about money.[27]

> There was once a prince who was seeking spiritual freedom.
>
> The man had left his privileged life and wandered in order to find answers to the suffering he saw around him. After a few years, he spent time with others who had a similar aim, to free themselves from suffering. They practised methods such as barely eating and extreme breathing techniques. Some would inflict physical pain on themselves. The man joined in. He came close to death on many occasions as he sought freedom from suffering and unhappiness.
>
> After five years, the man realised that, rather than freeing his mind from suffering, he now spent all his time thinking about nothing but suffering. He had spent so much time on his physical body that he had become obsessed with the very thing he was trying to escape from. This man was Gautama Buddha, a real man who lived some 2,500 years ago.

We should spend only as much time thinking about money as is necessary to not have to think about money.

Never is this more true than when we look at the impact of financial decisions on our physical health. As we have seen, thinking about money and the future is stressful. When we worry about money, either the lack of it or the responsibilities that it brings, this creates stress, which adversely affects our health.

This is a constant, ongoing process that we need to understand if we are going to have a healthier relationship with money.

THE ROLE OF IMMUNE CELLS IN YOUR BODY

At the Penny Brohn UK cancer centre, the staff provide support to people with cancer. They show a video to new clients. It is a video of human cells. Some of those cells are called 'immune cells.' There is one group of immune cells known by the more dramatic name of 'natural killer cells.' These roam around our bodies looking for cancer cells to destroy.

In the video, one of these immune cells comes across a cancer cell. It identifies the unwanted cell, injects it with poison and destroys it. You can easily look up similar videos online to see this happen for yourself. It is a quite extraordinary sight.

This is what immune cells do – they keep us healthy by 'policing' the bad cells.

When a person has a cancerous growth, Western medicine takes the approach of attacking the cancer cells with chemotherapy and radiotherapy. But, in addition, as they teach at the Penny Brohn UK centre, we should be providing support to the immune cells.

This basic principle is becoming the new medical phenomenon called 'lifestyle medicine' (also known as 'integrative medicine').

HAPPY MEANS HEALTHY

According to the British Society of Lifestyle Medicine, there are six areas we should particularly focus on in order to support our bodies:[28]

- Healthy eating
- Mental wellbeing (in particular reducing stress)
- Physical activity
- Healthy relationships
- Minimising harmful substances
- Sleep

Looking after each of these areas is obviously going to be beneficial, but equally so is avoiding the negative versions of each of them. Healthy eating, good. Processed food, bad.

One of these six areas is especially correlated with money – stress.

STRESS IS BAD FOR YOUR IMMUNE CELLS

If stress is bad for us, why does it exist? If evolution has done its job, then surely stress has a purpose?

'Stress' is a catch-all word for how our bodies react to fear. Stress raises our blood pressure, reduces our ability to digest food and brings on inflammation – all of which is designed to help the brain and body focus on a short-term threat. (This is a simplistic overview of the effect of stress on our bodies; for a longer introduction see *The Stress Solution* by Dr Rangan Chatterjee.[29])

When you are in a state of stress or are unhappy, cortisol is produced as a warning system to prepare us for danger. This causes *more* stress, which dampens the immune system.

This is the body's natural reaction to danger – the 'fight-or-flight' reaction. If our ancestors were out hunting and a wolf appeared, the brain would trigger the release of cortisol to set off our stress response so that we would take the appropriate action.

This is not so helpful, however, when the stress is being caused by a sickness that you want your body to be fighting. Or by a decision about money which might have long-term consequences.

If we experience stress over a longer period, these reactions can cause significant harm to our bodies. Long-term stress can exacerbate existing conditions such as heart disease, stroke, type 2 diabetes, indigestion and Alzheimer's, as well as leading to symptoms such as depression, lack of energy and loss of appetite.

Our stress response has evolved over millions of years of evolution. We are meant to feel stress – in short bursts. The modern Western life, however, brings about pressures and requires the sort of decision-making that results in long-term stress. And this is a major cause of ill health in the Western world.

With money at its heart.

LIFESTYLE MEDICINE

Stress leads to ill health. When we try to create financial plans but think about money with System 1 when we should use System 2, this is stressful.

There is, however, a converse to the above that can work in our favour. Happiness is healthy.

Being happy has a proven benefit for your health. There is a lot of research that could be referenced to back up this assertion.[30] Not only do happier people recover better, but they are also less prone to illness in the first place. And yet Western medicine gives such little time to this aspect of our health.

General practitioners (GPs) in the UK have just eight minutes allocated for each patient. This is despite the fact that "around 20% of patients consult GPs for problems that are primarily social rather than medical."[31] And yet, according to one survey, half of GPs said that "the time they spend on non-health issues helps them understand their local community."[32]

Unhappiness is bad for you. For example, in a Harvard study on happiness, people who reported being lonely died younger (do take the time to watch the TED Talk on this subject by the study's director, Robert Waldinger).[33]

'Lifestyle prescribing' is a term that describes how this is put into practice within a GP setting. Thanks to the work of pioneers such as Dr Mike Dixon and Dr Rangan Chatterjee, this is becoming a more accepted way of helping people to live a happier lifestyle, and therefore a healthier lifestyle.[34] To quote Dr Chatterjee, "We're all familiar with the idea that lifestyle can be the cause of disease. What's not common knowledge is that a change in lifestyle can also be the treatment and prevent us from getting sick in the first place."[35]

The science behind this underpins the work of the Penny Brohn UK cancer centre, whose staff are able to give patients something that is an extremely limited commodity in the NHS.

Time.

They help people (let's not call them 'patients' – a patient is just a person who is poorly, so let's call them 'people') to understand what is happening to their bodies. They give information and the time to help people understand what that information means for them. They help reduce the stress that is inevitable at such a difficult time.

When you are in a state of happiness or experiencing joy, your body is in a restive and restorative state, which boosts your immune cells. If we can establish a relationship with money where it serves us instead of controlling us, and take proactive measures to utilise it to create a more fulfilling life, then this can have a beneficial impact on our wellbeing.

And it's not just the immune cells. Strong negative emotions, such as anger and depression, are known to be directly related to cardiovascular causes of death, such as stroke and heart disease. There are many studies that have demonstrated a link between happiness and our health. For an excellent overview, see *Happiness: Unlocking the Mysteries of Psychological Wealth* by Ed Diener and Robert Biswas-Diener.[36]

Financial wellbeing, therefore, can help us to be happy in order to be healthy. A better relationship with money should mean less stress and thereby support the immune system.

CONCLUDING PART ONE

From this and the preceding chapters, the challenges in preparing
our financial wellbeing plan have become clear:
- The need to fund a period of no income arose extremely
  recently in human history
- We tend to view success as being linked to money
- Accumulating money has therefore become something
  we both strive for and need to do
- We struggle to see ourselves in the future
- We do not tend to delay gratification
- We make financial decisions with System 1
- We are not therefore programmed for financial planning
- As a result, money is a cause of stress
- Stress is bad for our health

Next, in *Part Two*, we will turn to the four cornerstones of financial wellbeing to look at what we can do to solve this conundrum.
How can we be better at financial planning, as defined by being
focused on our wellbeing, and therefore not induce stress.

How can we shift the emphasis of our relationship with money,
so that we can use it as a tool for our benefit, rather than being
controlled by it as our master?

PART 2

BUILDING YOUR FINANCIAL WELLBEING PLAN

●●●●

INTRODUCING THE FOUR CORNERSTONES OF FINANCIAL WELLBEING

We humans spend a lot of time and energy thinking about, researching and debating what makes us happy. We seem to have an endless fascination with our own minds.Philosophers, novelists, psychiatrists, artists, neuroscientists, academics, psychologists – all of us. Walk into any pub on an evening and you will probably find someone talking about whether they are happy, and why.

This is how I picture the current state of our understanding of happiness. I imagine a school disco. Typically, at the start of a school disco, dotted around the outside of the hall are several groups, each standing around sullenly, glaring at the others.

Leaning against one wall are the academics. They have insightful models of happiness, are doing cool research and producing fascinating research papers, and publishing books.

In one corner are the neuroscientists. They've spent years pinpointing in which part of the brain happiness happens. They are producing amazing papers and books that are giving us ever greater insight into the physiology of how happiness works in our brains.

In another corner are the behavioural finance experts. They often work with businesses and are excitedly developing theories about why we do things. They are applying their knowledge of what drives our behaviours in some cool ways (such as by helping to develop products and services that increase the wellbeing of customers) and some perhaps not so cool (such as by finding new ways to get customers to buy more stuff, or beat investment markets).

Then we have the financial advisers. A disparate group, some are rolling their eyes, saying that this isn't their responsibility. Others have their arms folded, saying they have been doing it for years (without actually taking the time to understand what 'it' is). Some, however, are listening carefully, excited to have new knowledge to apply to the financial planning process.

And then, in the final corner are the Buddhists. I picture them nonchalantly leaning against the wall, smiling, saying to anyone who will listen, "What are you all so excited about? We've been talking about this stuff for two and a half thousand years!"

Let us bring together strands from all of these various approaches in our understanding of happiness and its relationship to money, in order to provide one unifying approach.

THE FOUR CORNERSTONES OF FINANCIAL WELLBEING

The four cornerstones of financial wellbeing model has four parts:

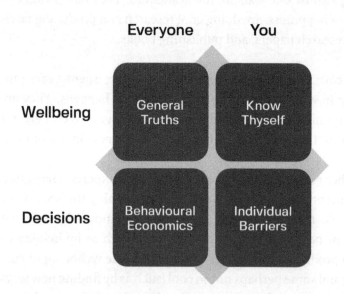

This book will help you to construct your own financial wellbeing plan by looking at these four areas of your wellbeing:

- What brings joy to anyone and everyone?
  We'll examine the research over many decades and what it tells us about how to be happy – the **general truths** of happiness.

- What brings joy uniquely to each of us?
  How can you **know thyself** so that your financial
  wellbeing plan will be unique to you?
- What are your financial beliefs?
  Our attitudes and beliefs around money are
  a major factor in our relationship to money,
  and can set up **barriers** to our wellbeing.
- What are your **behaviours**?
  We all have behavioural biases wired into us that
  may be resulting in poor financial decisions.

The four areas are interlinked because the desire to accumulate wealth is in contradiction to values aligned with wellbeing.[37]

These are the four cornerstones of our financial wellbeing plan. We will look at the latest research from psychology and academia, some of which is true of *everyone* and some of which will help you to identify behaviour that is unique to *you*. We will look at the sources of joy and *wellbeing*. And we will consider how we might make better financial *decisions* – which means financial decisions that will improve your wellbeing.

First, let us lay a few foundation stones and set out some important principles so that we can prepare the ground for our financial wellbeing plan.

● ● ● ●

GENERAL TRUTHS PART 1: THREE BASIC PRINCIPLES ABOUT MONEY

This book is about our relationship to money. It seeks to gain a better understanding of that relationship, in order that we can make improvements that will lead to a happier life. For many of us, this will need a shift in thinking to overcome some of our pre-conceptions and assumptions about money.

I'd like to establish three principles in order to lay a firm foundation on which we can build our financial wellbeing plan.

THE FIRST PRINCIPLE: WE ARE GOOD

The first guiding principle that I'd suggest we should use – that we *need* to use – might feel counter-intuitive at first. But it is a concept that, when I first read about it, I realised I really needed to hear.

Humans are fundamentally good.

As Nelson Mandela so rightly said, "No one is born hating another person because of the colour of his skin, or his back-ground, or his religion."[38] We have been taught to be the people that we are, and we have developed our values and beliefs from our experiences.

Our starting point, however, built into us from thousands of years of history, is to be good and kind.[39] Deviating from that first principle comes from influence and experience.

The trouble is, happiness doesn't sell. The daily news, social media, the movies and TV are all full of examples of humans being *un*kind. People being nice to each other, showing small acts of kindness, doesn't sell as well as news items about heartache and tragedy, or TV shows purporting to get into the minds of serial killers.

We tend to assume that, in a life-or-death situation, most people would take the 'every person for themselves' attitude and literally trample over each other trying to escape.

This is what we see every day on the news and in movies. In a disaster movie, an announcement from the government of, say, an alien invasion is accompanied by scenes of panic – shops being looted, cars crashing, people pushing each other aside to get to safety. We have been persuaded that the *Lord of the Flies* scenario – where, left to their own devices, a group of boys turn to aggression and violence – is the reality of the human condition.

In practice, this is not the norm. Example after example shows that people will be orderly, even helping complete strangers to get to safety before themselves, or jumping into rivers to save strangers at great risk to themselves.[40]

If we are born to be kind and good, then it follows that when we are less kind, it must be because something or someone is knocking us off our natural state. There might be many reasons for this – maybe we feel threatened, or we are defending our loved ones. Maybe we feel our rights are being impinged upon, or that there has been an injustice.

A person isn't a thing; we are a process.[41] If we can learn how to be bad, we can also learn how to be good. In doing so, we will find wellbeing.

If we accept the fundamental truth that humans are born to be good, then we should base our relationship with money upon this principle. Our financial wellbeing plan should help us to do the good things that we want to do. If you are tempted to use money in a way that is not conducive to your wellbeing, to your latent desire to be good, then it means something is trying to push you off that path.

> The legendary Hollywood actor Dustin Hoffman appeared on the interview programme *Wogan* in 1992. During a Q&A session, an audience member asked the actor about the roles he had played, many of which were repugnant, unpleasant characters (such as the pimp Ratso from *Midnight Cowboy*). How, went the question, did Mr Hoffman manage to play those characters with such compassion?
>
> Hoffman gave the most wonderful answer. He explained that, as he saw it, everyone has an inner dignity. No one does something because they know it is wrong. They do things for their own reasons. Everyone who does something that might be perceived as wrong will have an explanation for why they did it – a justification. All he tried to do as an actor, he said, was to find that reason, that personal dignity.

From this first principle that our relationship to money should foster our innate goodness, let us now consider a second founding principle. Is it actually possible to be happier? And, if it is, who controls this?

THE SECOND PRINCIPLE: 50% OF YOUR HAPPINESS IS IN YOUR CONTROL

What actually makes us happy? If we are unhappy, is it our fault or the fault of our circumstances? If we change our circumstances, will we automatically become happier?

The good news is that there are three elements to what determines our happiness levels.[42] And there is even better news: two of them can be changed.

THE SET POINT THEORY OF HAPPINESS

Set point theory says that we each have a certain level of happiness and that we return to that level irrespective of life events.[43]

Many of us travel through life accepting our lot, seeking happiness where we can. We might have times when we feel okay and other times when we feel sad. There will be short, temporary bursts where we might feel happy, although these are usually occasions rather than periods.

We have probably all known someone who could be described as 'happy being miserable.' Others seem to go through life with a smile on their faces.

Set point theory explains this. We each have our own level of happiness. We oscillate around our own personal set point, depending on what is going on in our lives at the time. Something good happens, and we might feel happier for a time before reverting back to our set point. Something bad happens, and we may feel low for a bit but we acclimatise to the new reality and move back to our set point (this is known as 'hedonic adaptation'). It takes something pretty major to make a permanent change to our set point (we'll be returning to set point theory in *Chapter 10*).

THE SOURCE OF YOUR SET POINT

This leads to an important question: what sets our set point? Early research suggested that our set point is inherited – it is genetic – and that our innate level of wellbeing is something we are given at birth.

Does this mean we cannot change our long-term happiness? More recent research suggests that your inherited level of happiness actually only accounts for **50% of your wellbeing** – which means you have 50% left to play with![44]

THINGS THAT HAPPEN *TO* YOU

If 50% of your set point is inherited, the second contributory factor to your level of happiness is your circumstances. Ask young people, for example, what will make them happy.[45] They might well reply that money and fame would be major contributors. Other circumstances – such as health, physical attractiveness, where we live and status – might intuitively feel like major factors in happiness. However, in fact, they make up only **10% of your wellbeing**.

Unlike our set point, these *are* factors that we can affect. They tend, however, to be the *only* thing we focus on – accumulation of wealth, buying a bigger house, moving to a nicer area, getting a better job. We often spend our lives – and our money – focusing on areas that actually only contribute *one tenth* of our total happiness levels.

INTENTIONAL HAPPINESS

The remaining **40% of your wellbeing** is down to you. It is your attitude, your "intentional activity"[46] – what you do, what you think, what you say.

There are many, many books about training the mind for happiness. These range from self-help books to daily affirmations to mindfulness to meditation to spiritual journeys. Two books that have helped me are *A Monk's Guide to Happiness* by Gelong Thubten and *A Pocket Guide to a Mindful Life* by Martin Stepek.[47] What we can take from this knowledge is that if we can control how we think and act, then we should spend and invest our money in ways that support this.

Our second foundation block, therefore, is to acknowledge that improving our wellbeing is within our control – but that we are probably looking in the wrong place. Rather than accumulating wealth, or just spending money to improve our circumstances, we should focus on our relationship to money and how we might change our intentional activities.

> **TIP FOR FINANCIAL ADVISERS:** If you want evidence that financial wellbeing is the future for financial planning and financial advice, then this section surely provides it.
>
> Only 10% of our happiness comes from accumulation of wealth, or getting a bigger house, or similar circumstances. A whopping 40% of happiness comes from our approach to life and how we respond to things.
>
> And yet the 10% tends to be the only focus of financial advice.

There are so many distractions in life that try to get us to focus on the things that don't matter (or, at best, only make up 10% of what matters). Financial advisers will need to take a proactive approach to financial wellbeing. Clients are unlikely to raise such issues with you. Advise the person, not just the money.

THE THIRD PRINCIPLE: MONEY AS AN OBJECTIVE LEADS TO UNHAPPINESS

There are some values that are universal, common to us all.[48] The priorities that each individual places on these values, however, are very different.

There are correlations between each of these values. Some values are correlated closely – such as *conformity* and *tradition*. Likewise, someone who likes *security* is also likely to score highly on measures of *conformity*.

Other values are, broadly speaking, opposite to each other. Someone who seeks personal *achievement* is unlikely to feel *benevolence*. Similarly, a person who seeks *power* is unlikely to care too much about *universalism* (the survival needs of others).

Professor Tim Kasser built on these principles by using a similar idea, but applying a range of personal goals rather than values.[49] His findings showed that some of those goals were well aligned. For example, someone who chose *safety* as a personal goal was also likely to choose *physical health*.

On the other hand, someone who saw *hedonism* (a devotion to pleasure) as a priority was likely to see *spirituality* as unimportant, and vice versa.

Crucially for financial wellbeing, two personal goals that were very closely aligned were opposite to two other personal goals that were themselves closely aligned. Someone who saw *financial success* and *popularity* as important personal goals saw *self-acceptance* and *community* as less important.

From this we can draw our third founding principle, that **a person who sees money as an objective is likely to be less happy than they might otherwise be.**

CONCLUSION

We can now start our financial wellbeing plan from a great position: we are designed to be good, we know that 50% of the control of our wellbeing resides within us, and we understand that accumulation of wealth is not an objective we should prioritise if we want to be happy.

Now we will look at how we make decisions, and what this tells us about improving our relationship to money.

CHAPTER 7

● ● ● ●

WHY WE DO WHAT WE DO

All the knowledge and education in the world won't get you to do something if you are not motivated to do it. There are things we know that we should do, and yet we don't. This is especially true when it comes to money.

In this chapter we'll look at what motivates us to do things, before applying this to our relationship with money. In this way we can become more motivated to spend our money to accumulate life, not the other way around.

WHAT MOTIVATES US

Think about jobs you have carried out in the past – these might be chores around the house, helping run a local club, perhaps being a school governor, or paid employment. You will have been motivated to do some of these jobs but less motivated to carry out others. Whether (or how much) you were paid won't always have been the main factor in this motivation. You will probably have performed the jobs you were motivated to do better than the others. You almost certainly enjoyed those jobs more.

What brought about this difference in motivation?

This question has particular relevance to major life and financial decisions, such as retirement or job changes. If a current job is not satisfying, why might that be? And what would need to change in order for you to be more motivated? In retirement, what might get you out of bed with a spring in your step?

Self-determination theory is a psychological explanation for why we are motivated to do some things more than others.[50] As we saw in brief in *Chapter 1*, this theory says that we are motivated to do something when three key elements are in place. These are:

- Competence (the ability to do the thing)
- Relatedness (connection with others, including our future selves)
- Autonomy (being able to control our destiny and behaviours)

If these three parts of self-determination theory are in place, we feel motivated and happy. If they are not, this leads to a lack of motivation, unhappiness and even to mental health issues.

Note that this is not black and white – these three part are not either present or not present. We don't either have or not have motivation to do something. If we can get *more* competence, for example, we will be *more* motivated. Let's look at these in a bit more detail.

COMPETENCE

First, competence means being good at something, but it's more than just having ability or talent. It's about being good enough at a thing that gives you purpose. You want to be at least competent enough to be able to control the outcome.

This is especially true of money. In order to be motivated to engage with your finances, you need to feel that you will be competent in doing so.

Back in *Chapter 3* we saw how we deal with money decisions from a position of fear, because our brains aren't built to think about such long-term issues. Competence around money is therefore a very difficult thing to achieve.

One solution to the competence question is to engage an expert, such as a financial planner. Competence doesn't need to just come from yourself – it can come from a combination of sources.

This can build on your own knowledge to increase your competence. See *Appendix 3: How Do I Find a Financial Adviser Who Is Right for Me?* for some tips on how to find the right financial advice for you.

RELATEDNESS

We will be more motivated to do something if it includes a sense of connectedness to others. This might be helping someone else, working with someone else or some other form of impact.

This aligns with the Harvard study mentioned in *Chapter 4* which found that the quality of social relationships is the largest contributor to our happiness.[51] Not only do social relationships make a big difference to our wellbeing, but it also turns out that they are a basic part of us wanting to do something in the first place.

Relatedness also means having a sense of being part of something beyond ourselves, to have meaning and purpose.

When we relate this aspect of motivation to our relationship to money, we need to ask who it is we are connecting with. When it comes to savings, pensions and so on, we are creating a benefit for our future selves. This is a challenge to which we will return.

AUTONOMY

Finally, we have autonomy. This is the feeling that you are able to take charge of your own destiny and behaviours.

Autonomy includes living a life that is compatible with what you believe. For example, if your job allows you to make decisions but what the company actually *does* is not aligned with your personal beliefs and purpose, then you're unlikely to be very motivated –

or happy, for that matter. You may have control over your daily work, but not over the impact that this has.

This is a reason why accumulating wealth doesn't add to your long-term wellbeing – if you are going to be rewarded for doing something with money, but the thing that you are doing is not something that makes you proud, then you aren't going to get much wellbeing from doing it.

This explains why certain jobs attract very high earnings but others (such as nursing) can be paid poorly. The pay for jobs that deliver little in the way of purpose needs to be that much higher than jobs which deliver large amounts of purpose.

Money is not the only motivator when doing a job. Saying 'thank you' or 'well done' to someone when they have done a good job will make them feel that they are in control of what they do, and therefore increase their feeling of autonomy – as well as competence and relatedness, as it happens. Offering someone a financial reward or target if they achieve a purposeful task might even reduce their motivation.[52]

APPLYING SELF-DETERMINATION THEORY TO MONEY

Thinking about self-determination theory in relation to money can provide a quick path to identifying improvements.

For example, it can help us to be motivated to make financial plans. If we spend time working out what we would like to do that gives us control, uses our skills and abilities, brings us into a community, and brings us meaning and purpose, we might see our future selves more clearly. This in turn is likely to encourage us to save more.

BEING PULLED, NOT PUSHED

Self-determination theory can be instructive at moments of change, such as selling a business, changing job or location, or retirement. In a career, you have a role to play: people need you or look to you for advice or to access your expertise. You might have reached a position where you have a degree of control – autonomy – over what you do. Perhaps you are seen as being knowledgeable and therefore have competence, and you work with colleagues and so have relatedness.

Then you retire, or sell your business, and suddenly all of that is gone. How are you going to replace those connections, that sense of purpose from being in control of your work, and the respect you received from others?

Darren had worked all his life for a major bank. He had enjoyed his job and liked his colleagues. In his spare time, he satisfied his need for creativity by developing his skills in making stained-glass windows.

In his fifties, Darren received financial planning advice. As a result, he took early retirement from the bank. He didn't want to stop working and couldn't afford to not earn, but equally he didn't need the same level of income. He set up a small studio in his back garden and began exhibiting his stained-glass windows at local craft fairs. Pretty soon he was earning again – nowhere near as much as he had at the bank, but enough to justify his decision to retire from his job.

There is evidence that demonstrates this importance of identifying autonomy, competence and relatedness through planning before retirement, and how it leads to a more fulfilled retirement.

One research project showed that retirees had higher levels of motivation from knowledge, stimulation and accomplishment, rather than extrinsic activities such as travel. It also suggested that both accomplishment and stimulation were positively related to satisfaction in retirement. Finding meaning and purpose in retirement was a bigger contributor than other factors, even health.[53]

A study of 9,050 people in England who had an average age of 65 when the study began found that those who reported having a sense of purpose over the ensuing 8.5 years were less likely to die within that period.[54]

The measure that the study used to assess the degree of purpose is 'eudemonic wellbeing.' This means the feeling that what you do is worthwhile. Those in the highest category of this definition of wellbeing lived on average two years longer than those in the lowest category.

Working out what you want from your future, then creating a plan to get there, will mean that the next phase of life will be pulling you towards it. This is considerably more exciting than having the feeling that you are being pushed away from where you currently are.

CONCLUSION

Finding autonomy, competence and relatedness with money will increase our motivation to engage and create financial plans that will bring wellbeing both now and in the future.

Using money to enable us to live a life of meaning and purpose will, according to self-determination theory, allow us to be much more motivated to engage with our financial plan. Referring back to the three-step plan in *Chapter 1*, understanding Steps Two (understand that happiness comes from within) and Three (be compassionate) will inspire us to take Step One (create a financial wellbeing plan for a happy future)!

Let's now take some time to understand where wellbeing comes from. This should give us a better knowledge of what we mean by 'meaning and purpose,' and so increase our competence, relatedness and autonomy from money.

CHAPTER 8

• • • •

GENERAL TRUTHS PART 2: MEANING AND PURPOSE

So far, this book has laid out three important principles: we are inherently good; our attitudes affect our wellbeing; and money as an objective makes us unhappy.

We have also recognised that living a purposeful and meaningful life, while developing a positive relationship with money where we see it as a tool for our benefit instead of a controlling master, can enhance our overall wellbeing.

We now have some criteria which we can use to assess our financial decisions. Next, let's look at some other principles of happiness and examine what we mean by 'meaning and purpose' in greater detail.

DOES MONEY MAKE US HAPPY?

Let's answer the most common question people ask about money: does it make us happy?

The answer is a simple one: yes – and no!

If we have nothing, then some money will increase our wellbeing. But there comes a point where *more* money does not make you *more* happy. One study suggested that earnings above $95,000 per year (at 2018 values) would not lead to an increase in wellbeing.[55] Although the details behind this figure are arguable, to do so rather misses the importance of the finding. There comes a point after which more money doesn't make you any *more* happy. And that point may well be a lot lower than many of us might have guessed.

As we have seen from the fact that we can affect 50% of our wellbeing (see *Chapter 6*), asking whether money makes you happy or not is to miss the point of money. It is your *attitude to money* that affects your wellbeing. The things that bring wellbeing are invariably not directly linked to money. Money might bring wellbeing or it might not. It depends on our attitude towards it.

THE FIVE ELEMENTS OF WELLBEING WE CAN INFLUENCE

There are a number of ways of looking at happiness and wellbeing. We will use a model which outlines five "elements [that form] the currency of a life that matters."[56]

The five elements that make up our wellbeing and that we can *do something about* are:

- Career (how you occupy your time)
- Social (your close relationships)
- Financial (your relationship with money)
- Physical (having the energy to get things done)
- Community (your engagement with others where you live and work)

There are several aspects of these five elements of wellbeing that are worthy of note.[57]

Firstly, what matters most is the balance between these five elements. There is no *right* balance, however; this will be a little different for each of us. The important principle is that an imbalance between two or more elements will reduce overall wellbeing.

For example, someone who focuses too heavily on career wellbeing may find that they are in a highly paid but highly stressful job, and that this is affecting their health. They may have poor relationships with their colleagues as they all scrabble to the top of the pile. They may wake up one day and realise that they missed their children's younger years through being in the office late each day. And yet to others they may seem very successful.

Someone who needs a strong community may rank this as more important than physical exercise. Our health, however, will always be important.

One of the five may be more important to you than the others, but they are *all* important. You might want to take a moment to consider what balance between these five elements of wellbeing would be ideal for you. You might do this on your own, then perhaps compare the results with your partner's if applicable. Is there a joint optimum level you might come up with? Exercise 4 in *Appendix 1: Your Financial Wellbeing Plan* will help you to identify and assess your wellbeing in these areas.

Secondly, although the balance between the five is key, there is one that is more important that the others: social wellbeing.

The previously mentioned Harvard study on happiness has been tracking what contributes to wellbeing for many decades now, and the quality of social relationships has emerged as the largest contributor to wellbeing.[58]

Not *quantity*, note – but the *quality* of social relationships.

Thirdly, of those five elements, I'd suggest there is one that influences the others, rather than directly contributing to our overall wellbeing: financial.

Satisfaction with the social, community, physical and career aspects of our lives directly contributes to living a life with meaning and purpose. However, as we saw in the previous chapter, a focus on money not only does not contribute to our wellbeing – it can actively work against it.

In some ways this gives us another definition of financial wellbeing. It is concerned with how our relationship with money contributes to – or detracts from – our overall level of wellbeing.

MONEY AND HAPPINESS

There are five parts of the relationship between money and happiness, which I referred to as the five pillars of financial wellbeing in *The Financial Wellbeing Book* (a model based on the Consumer Financial Protection Bureau's report *Financial Well-being: The Goal of Financial Education* and subsequently adopted by the Institute of Financial Wellbeing).[59] These five pillars are:

- A clear path to identifiable objectives
- Being able to cope with financial shocks
- Having financial options
- Control of daily finances
- Clarity and security for those that we leave behind

The Financial Wellbeing Book looked at these pillars in detail, and you will find exercises that cover these pillars in *Appendix 1: Your Financial Wellbeing Plan*.

To repeat my favourite saying: financial planning is really very simple: you simply work out what you want from life then spend your money on that. We might argue that the first of these five pillars, 'a clear path to identifiable objectives,' *is* financial planning. The 'clear path' part is almost certainly a cashflow forecast, a wonderful tool used by all good financial planners.

'Identifiable objectives' requires a lot more investigation, however. What are these objectives that we are aiming for?

INTERNAL AND EXTERNAL SELF-WORTH

To ease us into a better definition of what we might mean by an objective, let's consider the question of where our self-worth comes from.

TIP FOR FINANCIAL ADVISERS: For many years it has been necessary to start any recommendation by establishing the client's objectives. The most common objective that you see in a suitability letter is along the lines of "Your objective is to beat inflation with your investments by accessing our portfolios." I've spoken to many a compliance department about this, and they estimate that some 95% of files they check have this same objective.

But this isn't really an objective: it is an outcome.

An improvement might be "Your objective is to retire at the age of X." This, however, is a goal, something that is finite.

A financial wellbeing approach would be to state objectives in terms of intrinsic motivations, possibly with goals that will lead to a life with meaning and purpose. For example: "To reach a sufficient level of financial security that would allow me to change career from banking to making stained glass windows".

In the three-step guide to happiness that began this book, I talked about understanding that joy comes from within, from having self-worth.

I'd like to provide an illustration of the danger of relying on external sources for our wellbeing with a very personal story. It also shows the danger of relying on money and status as sources of self-worth and wellbeing.

My father was a financial adviser. He came from very working-class beginnings – his father was, among other jobs, a road sweeper.

Dad worked hard throughout his life, progressing up the greasy corporate ladder, until a redundancy led to him becoming a self-employed financial adviser. For a few years he did pretty well, and he enjoyed some of the trappings of this success. This included buying his dream car – a second-hand Jaguar Sovereign. He also bought an expensive Bang & Olufsen stereo and a soda stream.

Don't underestimate the social value of a soda stream in Somerset in the 1980s! For some reason this became a symbol of uninhibited decadence among my friends. That soda stream was constantly brought up as supposed proof that I thought I was better than everyone else (not that this stopped my friends from coming round and enjoying its fizzy, sticky delights).

Dad was happy: he had friends, his income was good and, especially in late 1980s Britain, this brought the respect of others. Things were rosy.

There were two things, however, that we didn't know.

The first was that things were not quite as good as he would have had his friends and family believe. There was a recession in the early 1990s. In particular, house prices crashed. After a period of rapidly rising prices and easy-to-get mortgages requiring minimal deposits, negative equity became common. The recession hit hard, and my father's business was one of those that suffered.

Eventually, my father went bankrupt. I had left home by then, but my parents lost their house, their car, almost everything. We only found out that Dad – a proud man – was in financial trouble long after it was too late to help. Not wanting to worry us, he suffered in silence.

My father was never the same. Certain 'friends' abandoned him, and his pride – his sense of self-worth – took a hit from which it never recovered.

Where does self-worth come from? There are two types of self-worth: one that comes from what we *have* (perhaps possessions, perhaps status) and the other from what we *are* (from simply being human and being connected with other humans).[60]

This was the second thing I didn't know. My father's *self-worth* had been entirely derived from his *net worth*.[61] As long as he was earning well – and visibly – then his self-worth was strong. But as soon as the source of his income disappeared, his status and therefore his pride disappeared with it. His self-worth never recovered.

ACHIEVABLE INTRINSIC MOTIVATIONS

Research has found that only one in five people are very aware of what makes their life enjoyable. Only 15% are aware of what makes it meaningful.[62] And yet we have identified that living a life with meaning and purpose is key to our wellbeing.

Another way of looking at self-worth is to return to self-determination theory, which describes two types of motivation.[63]

An *extrinsic* motivation is something you do for external reasons. Maybe it is applause, or wealth, or status; to meet a deadline, or achieve a target or reward. Perhaps it is to avoid punishment.

An *intrinsic* motivation is something you do just for its inherent satisfaction. If you find it difficult to explain why you want to achieve something (you just *do*), it could be because of an intrinsic motivation.

The happiness we get from extrinsic motivations is temporary – that happiness lasts only as long as the applause lasts. In the case of my father, for example, it lasted only as long as the money was there to buy the status items.

Achieving intrinsic motivations, on the other hand, leads to a life with meaning and purpose. This gives us internal self-worth, which brings about longer-lasting wellbeing as it is not reliant upon others. It gives us greater control over our own self-worth.

There is, however, one more twist in the tale of intrinsic motivations.

THE LOSS AVERSION KICKER

Loss aversion is a behavioural bias that we all carry with us. In short, we feel the loss of something greater than how much we feel the equivalent gain.

Imagine losing something important. A wedding ring, maybe, or a wallet or purse. You curse and swear – maybe there are tears.

A week later, you find the thing down the back of the sofa. There is relief – but the intensity of the emotion is not to the same level as when you first thought you'd lost the item.

Or maybe you look at the stock market and see that your investments have gone down by 20%. Your reaction will be considerably stronger than if you see that your investments have gone up by 20%.

Research by behavioural expert Neil Bage shows that we feel the loss of something 3.69 times greater than we feel the equivalent gain.[64]

Now, let's turn back to our motivations. If we set ourselves on a path to achieve intrinsic motivations, but we *fail* to achieve them, there is a real danger that we will make ourselves much less happy – 3.69 times less happy! – than if we achieved the motivation.

And so it is for this reason that our financial plans need to aim for achievable intrinsic motivations. We might, therefore, update the first of our pillars of financial wellbeing to:

A clear path to achievable intrinsic motivations

REWARDS

I touched earlier on an interesting side issue about the nature of rewards. If we receive an *extrinsic* reward for an *intrinsic* motivation, it can actually *reduce* the motivation. If someone gives their time for a charity but then is given money for doing so, they may well actually stop giving up their time. It has become a job; the feeling of doing good disappears, and they become less motivated.

If we set up our financial wellbeing plan to give extrinsic rewards, therefore, we are far less likely to engage with it. In contrast, if we create our financial wellbeing plan to help us achieve a life with meaning and purpose, then our overall motivation to engage with our finances will go up.[65]

CONCLUSION

Living a life with meaning and purpose is a great source of well-being, and this is more likely to come from intrinsic motivations. We have also established that our relationship with money will be improved when we adopt an approach based more on internal self-worth than external factors.

These are principles that are true of all of us. The next question to consider, the second of our four cornerstones of financial wellbeing, is: what are *your* achievable intrinsic motivations?

• • • •

CHAPTER 9

FINDING YOUR INTRINSIC MOTIVATIONS

What brings us wellbeing? Some answers are the same for all of us. A good meal. Sunshine on the skin. Time spent with loved ones.

In this chapter, however, we seek something that can be a little harder to find. We are looking for things that bring *you* wellbeing. To identify *your* intrinsic motivations. Watching sport will bring joy to many people. Watching cricket will bring joy to only those who like cricket. And watching a five-day test match that ends in a draw is something that brings joy to only a select few of us!

Happiness is like trying to balance a chicken on your nose. It can be done, but it doesn't tend to last very long. Achieving extrinsic motivations brings about only short-term bursts of happiness, because these motivations come from external sources.

We are seeking those *achievable intrinsic motivations* that will provide longer-lasting wellbeing. Living a life with meaning and purpose will help to maintain your set point of wellbeing (see *Chapter 6*).

As we go through the characteristics of motivations, you may want to reflect back on your definition of success. Is it based on goals or motivations? Are they intrinsic or extrinsic? How is your relationship with money helping or hindering the achievement of your intrinsic motivations?

THE DANGER OF GOALS (THEN WHAT HAPPENS?)

When people want to achieve something, they often begin by defining their destination in terms of goals. The world of motivational quotes is littered with the importance of setting, and achieving, goals. There is, however, one significant issue with aiming at goals – they are finite. Once a goal has been achieved, then what happens?

Take retirement, for example. Perhaps you have a goal to retire at a certain age. Suppose you achieve that goal. Then what happens?

A focus on setting and achieving goals can lead to unhappiness if it is not accompanied by a wider sense of purpose that relates to the time after the goal has been achieved. For example, there are many, many stories of sports professionals who achieved their goal of winning a trophy or gold medal, only to emotionally crash afterwards.

> One of the ultimate goals must surely be to win an Olympic gold medal. It takes total dedication to be the best in the world, which is what is required to achieve that goal.
>
> But then what happens?
>
> In all too many cases, the athlete experiences a breakdown. Michael Phelps, for example, has been open about considering suicide shortly after winning four gold medals at the 2012 Olympic Games in London.[66]
>
> Thankfully, this has been recognised, and help is at hand. The English Institute of Sport has a programme that it calls Performance Decompression. Dr Kate Hays is quoted on the organisation's website: "This hopefully provides the opportunity to reflect on and recognise what has been experienced, gain a sense of closure, and facilitate a smoother transition to what comes next."[67]

Our modern society has a preoccupation with 'goals' and 'targets.' Yet when we achieve a goal, we realise that we need to find another goal to work towards. Wellbeing isn't a goal. It's a state of mind.

How we accumulate and spend our money is a great example of the dissatisfaction that arises from chasing goals. Once you have that shiny new thing, your thoughts turn to the next shiny new thing. As our income goes up, so we allow ourselves more of those luxuries. Our focus moves from buying things we *need* to buying things we *want*. There is even a name for this phenomenon: lifestyle creep. We just never seem to have enough.

Collecting art is one visible way of demonstrating your extreme wealth. But does it ever stop? Can you ever own 'enough' art? Can the desire to own famous works of art ever be satisfied?

Hedge fund manager and billionaire Michael Steinhardt owned a huge art collection. In 2021 he was forced to surrender 180 works of art from his collection that had been stolen and illegally smuggled, valued at around $70 million. He had bought the art "without concern for the legality of his actions, the legitimacy of the pieces he bought and sold, or the grievous cultural damage he wrought across the globe" (according to the Manhattan District Attorney).[68]

FINANCIAL TECHNOLOGY AND GOALS

There are a huge number of apps and other types of financial technology that purport to help you manage your money. A lot of this 'fintech' (as it has become known) is built around achieving financial goals, which invariably means buying something.

These will typically include buying a car, a house or a dream holiday. But who is to say buying a house is something that everyone should do? There may be some people who would prefer to travel or move around with job changes, and for whom buying a house could be the worst thing they could do.

Financial goals can be either intrinsic or extrinsic. For example, wanting a boat because your friends have a boat would be an example of an extrinsic goal. Wanting a boat because sailing is your favourite pastime is a much more intrinsic goal.

Goals can also be necessary to reach something deeper. An example might be a savings goal that enables a person to change job to one that pays less but brings them greater purpose. But having financial goals *without* that deeper understanding of intrinsic motivations can make you less happy as you continue to chase goal after goal.

Technology that helps you plan and achieve financial goals only addresses one small part of the picture. And it might not be the part that will result in increasing your wellbeing (there is more on this in *Appendix 4: A Note For Financial Advisers*).

GOALS FOR BUSINESS OWNERS

As a financial planner, and latterly as a specialist in the Employee Ownership Trust, I have worked with many owners of small businesses. They often possess the vision that entrepreneurs are encouraged to have: dedicated and focused on building their businesses, with the ultimate aim of selling.

I have also seen many a business owner stay in their business for longer than was good for either them *or* the business. This is almost always because their business defined them – they had taken no time to think about what really brought them purpose. Or how to replace it.

The directors of Spotton Leeds were getting frustrated because their founder and current chair, Graham Spotton, wouldn't retire.[69] Then in his late sixties, he continued to go into the office and would attend various meetings, even when not specifically invited.

As one director put it, he liked to "lob in grenades" – he would listen to the meeting, then ask difficult questions, and watch with delight as the team struggled to answer them.

The directors wanted him to retire partly so that they could take over, but also so that they could buy his shares.

I was chatting with one of the directors and asked her why he wouldn't retire. She replied, "Because today, he's Graham Spotton, chair of Spotton Leeds. As soon as he retires, he's just Graham Spotton."

Maybe an offer does come in for the business. This is a highly stressful time for any business owner but, hopefully, all goes well and they sell.

And then what?

Sometimes, achieving a goal can take up so much mental energy that we are *unable* to think beyond it. This is very common in business owners, who are commonly so consumed with building, running, then selling their business that they forget to think about what happens next.

A business owner I was working with had been given a target by a previous business adviser that profit needed to be 30% of the company's turnover The business was going through a growth phase at the time, and the owner was working almost seven full days a week. He was very near to a nervous breakdown.

I questioned the reason for the focus on growth and the 30% target, the big goal he had been given. He could not explain why, just that it was the target and that he was single-mindedly focused on it.

I pointed out that the business had invested in new employees and that, during such a period, profit was bound to be down. Besides which, he was still making a profit of 20% of turnover, after all costs and his salary. He was earning a significant amount of money. How much did he actually need for his own financial plans?

He had never worked out this figure. He was too busy trying to get back to 30% profit.

The question to ask yourself is not "How much is my business worth?" but "How much do I *need* it to be worth?" Exercise 7 in *Appendix 1: Your Financial Wellbeing Plan* is specifically for business owners.

BEWARE THE BUCKET LIST

This idea of achieving financial goals is often framed by the expression "achieving your bucket list." It means ticking off a list of things you want to do before you die.

Probably the most common answer people give when asked what they want to do in retirement is that they would like to travel.

Perhaps visit Disneyland, or walk the Inca Trail to Machu Picchu. However, once you've returned from that dream holiday, then what happens?

> Last year two of my friends separately walked the Camino de Santiago, the pilgrim trail into Spain.
>
> One of them took the journey to discover himself. He did the whole trail of 500 miles over five weeks, alone. He spoke to other travellers in the evenings, sharing their life stories and comparing their reasons for taking the trail. On his return, he felt that he was a different person from the one that had left. He made some major life changes, including moving to a new area for a fresh start.
>
> The other went with a group of friends. They went to be able to say that they had 'done' the Camino. They walked the shortest version of the trail possible, around 65 miles. They are now planning their next walking challenge.

An interesting exercise might be to write down your list of things you've always wanted to do, your bucket list. Are they goals – things that, once done, can be ticked off? Or are they motivations – things that might provide longer-lasting wellbeing? Ideally they will be a blend of the two.

Ask yourself why each item is on your list. Are they extrinsic, something to please other people? Or are they intrinsic, something you might find hard to explain? Compare your conclusions with your definition of success. Does this enable you to amend or update your definition?

Rather than thinking about goals as being something we aim for, it might be more helpful to think of goals as also being steps on the way to finding meaning and purpose.

GOALS AND RETIREMENT

Before spending time working out our goals, we might first try to understand our intrinsic motivations. The goals which will get us there may then seem clearer.

For example, we can use the idea of having both motivations and goals to rethink retirement. Rather than retirement being a goal to be achieved in its own right, retirement can be a time for seeking and living with meaning and purpose.

Retirement does not mean what it used to mean. It no longer needs to be a time when we stop working. Instead, maybe we could think of it as a period of our lives when we move from working at something because we *have* to, to working at something because we *want* to.

This might mean not retiring per se, but a career change. Perhaps leaving a highly paid but stressful job for a lower-paid but more purposeful and enjoyable job. It could involve retiring and taking up a voluntary role where you can have greater impact. Maybe it's a move into consultancy, where you have flexibility in who you choose to work for.

IDENTIFYING WHAT MAKES YOU HAPPY

Now that we have identified some of the traps that await us when looking for a life with meaning and purpose, we can turn our attention to identifying our intrinsic motivations.

TIP FOR FINANCIAL ADVISERS: You can have an important role to play in helping clients to 'know thyself.' However, it is crucial to appreciate that this is unlikely to be something that comes naturally to you.

We are trained to solve problems. All through school and on to professional exams, we are given problems and expected to reduce the options until there is only one left – the answer.

When helping a client to find their intrinsic motivations, you need to do the opposite – to create more options. This will not come naturally, as you will be tempted to provide solutions.

Professional qualifications in the UK have no element of training in active listening and questioning. I strongly believe that every financial adviser and planner should undertake training in coaching skills – in listening and questioning.[70]

There is a difference between what makes us happy and what we pay attention to; a difference between how we spend our time and the things that we think will make us happy. In many ways, the gap between the two defines our wellbeing. As Paul Dolan says in *Happiness by Design*, "The production process for happiness is therefore how you allocate your attention."[71]

We could extend this statement to say that your wellbeing comes from how you allocate your money. Money is a currency that we can use to buy time. How we choose to spend our time is the key to finding our motivations.

FINDING YOUR PURPOSE

Living a life with meaning and purpose is not necessarily something that will happen in a flash of realisation. It might come from small changes, such as volunteering at a sports club that your children attend, or helping at a charity whose purpose you can relate to. Sometimes it *does* involve a big life moment, such as a change in job, but it can equally come in incremental steps.

So, let's just dial back a little here. Wellbeing comes from living a life with meaning and purpose – but this doesn't mean that everything you do must be meaningful or purposeful! That would be exhausting. We need to earn a living and we need to put food on the table.

We should have *something* in our lives that gives us meaning and purpose. One way of testing whether this is the case is to ask ourselves a question. Am I doing something in my life that is:
- Important to me?
- Important to someone else?
- Or important to everyone?[72]

Neil Gaiman gave a fabulous Commencement speech at the University of the Arts in 2012, "Make Good Art." This can be watched in full on YouTube.[73]

Gaiman included a piece of advice about what to do if you just don't know what to do. When you are stuck with a problem and you don't know the best course of action, just think of somebody who would know the answer and do what they would do.

This sounds a bit like a joke, but try it – it really works!

Exercises 8 and 9 in *Appendix 1: Your Financial Wellbeing Plan* will help you think about what purpose in your life means for you. It is, however, difficult to challenge our own assumptions. For this reason, you may well want to engage the help of a third party, such as a partner, friend, financial adviser or planner (who will preferably have undertaken coaching training), or coach.

IDENTIFYING YOUR CORE VALUES

Your core values give you the basis for what you would want your life to be like – in other words, a life that allows you to be true to those values. Our core values are the principles that make us who we are. See Exercise 10, on identifying your values, in *Appendix 1: Your Financial Wellbeing Plan.*

Your values are the non-negotiables in your life. They might change slowly over time, but you will not give them up readily. If you do, it is likely to make you unhappy.

Values are not aspirational. Be realistic and challenge yourself. If you put 'honesty' as one of your values, think about your recent past. Are there any times when you were not honest? If your partner asked if they looked nice in a particular item of clothing, did you lie so as not to upset them? This is because to be honest in this instance may have disregarded another value, such as compassion. You may therefore need to refine what it is you mean by 'honesty'. Do you mean 'candour' or 'integrity', for example?

Once you have identified your core values, you should have a clearer idea of who you are – and who you want to carry on being in the future.

CREATING THE CONDITIONS FOR WELLBEING

We need to create the conditions in our lives that will allow these values to appear and therefore enable us to find wellbeing.[74] Consider an aquarium of the kind that you might have at home, full of tropical fish. If you want the aquarium to thrive, then you need to look after the water, not the fish.

You may therefore wish to test your current situation, as well as your future plans, against your core values. Are you creating the right conditions for you to flourish?

YOU ARE WHAT YOU SAY YOU ARE

We have seen how we can struggle to take action now to benefit our future selves, because this feels like helping someone else. This is going to be exacerbated if we imagine our future selves to be very different to how we are now. One method of connecting to your future self, therefore, might be to start thinking about who you want to be in the present tense.

For example, a few years ago, after I had sold Ovation Finance, the financial planning business I had founded, I was at a party. Someone asked me what I did, and I was struggling to answer. I blustered about Ovation and about employee ownership, and mentioned that I had recently published my fourth book.

"Oh," they said. "So you're an author."

From then on I introduced myself as an author. Because if that's what I say I am, then that is what I am!

> Jeff Tweedy is the singer and songwriter for the American alt country band Wilco. He wrote an excellent book called *How to Write One Song*.[75]
>
> In it he describes how, as a child, he would tell people that he was a songwriter. He couldn't remember how that particular profession got into his head; he just thought it sounded cool.
>
> Then, after a few years of this, he thought he had better actually write some songs so that what he had been telling people was true. Then, he really was a songwriter. You are what you say you are!

ACHIEVING CLARITY WITH CASHFLOW FORECASTING

What might prevent such a change, from striving to achieve goals to uncovering motivations? How can you know what is possible?

As highlighted by the three-step approach outlined in *Chapter 1*, and the need to start with Step Two, one of the main blockages to freeing up our thinking about the future is a financial one. We are often so busy achieving short-term financial goals that we don't take time to step back and see where we are headed.

This is where cashflow forecasting can help – taking your financial position and projecting it forwards. Financial planners will use comprehensive cashflow software and a range of metrics around tax, inflation, investment returns, and so on to create a picture of your financial future.

But we're not just talking about a projection of where you are today. The real strength of cashflow forecasting lies in scenario modelling. What would you like your future to look like? What age are you going to be able to stop work? Could you accept a drop in salary to do a more meaningful job? Could you afford to set up your own business?

Even if you have a cashflow forecast, have you asked it the question you may have always wanted to ask? What would you *really* like to do next, that would give you real purpose – and can you afford to do it? This is a question that any financial planner should be able to answer for you with cashflow forecasting. See *Appendix 3: How Do I Find a Financial Adviser Who Is Right for Me?* for more about this.

HAPPINESS OR WELLBEING?

One way of testing whether your intrinsic motivation will provide meaning is to ask this question: will doing that thing bring you happiness or wellbeing?

In the book *The Art of Happiness*, Howard C. Cutler provides an example.[76] He tells of a woman who works as a counsellor to young offenders. She doesn't like living in the city, however. She gets a job offer working with adults in a small town, a place she has longed to live. She can't decide whether to accept the offer.

The book questions whether the move would give her happiness or wellbeing. The happiness would come from living in a beautiful house in an idyllic town. Wellbeing, however, would come from working with young people. Ultimately, this enables her to make the decision to stay in her current job.

TIP FOR FINANCIAL ADVISERS: When a client comes to you as a financial adviser or planner, what they say they want from you is often not what they actually want from you. For example, if a client says, "I'd like you to review and maybe consolidate my pensions," what they really mean might be, "I'm doing a job that doesn't align with my values but that pays very well, with a manager I don't like. I think I might be depressed, and I'd really like to change my job but don't know if I can afford to take a pay cut."

If a client arrives seeking investment advice or a pension review, the adviser or planner surely has a duty to ask a follow-up question to get to the heart of what those returns would give them. This might be: "What might your investments enable you to do?"[77]

CONCLUSION

Hopefully, if you have completed the exercises in *Appendix 1* I've mentioned, you will now have a better idea of what brings *you* wellbeing – what a life with meaning and purpose means to *you*. This should not be considered 'finished.' You might try something and discover it's not really for you. That's okay – you always have the right to change your mind!

Hopefully, however, you now have a better idea of what brings you wellbeing – and therefore whether your relationship with money is helping you to achieve this.

In order to help you with this process of refining and reassessing, we will now look at some more research about what makes us happy and the role that money takes.

●●●●

CHAPTER 10

GENERAL TRUTHS PART 3: THE REALITY OF HAPPINESS

We have reached the stage in our financial wellbeing process where achievable intrinsic motivations are firmly placed at its heart. You have started to understand what brings meaning and purpose to your own life. With the help of a financial planner and cashflow forecasting, you can plot a pathway towards that future.[78] You are now in a position to start to use your money to accumulate life, rather than the other way around.

To help you along this pathway and to provide a deeper understanding, let's look at some more of the research on happiness. This will help you to continue to refine your financial wellbeing plan.

THE BIOLOGY OF HAPPINESS

There are four chemicals in the brain that are sometimes known as the 'happy hormones.'

First we have **endorphins**, chemicals that are produced from exercise and other activities, including laughter and meditation. They relieve stress and pain, and can even give a mild high. On the downside, that can become something we chase.

Dopamine is known as the 'feel-good chemical.' We get dopamine when we achieve things, no matter how small. This is one explanation for why having a clear path to *achievable* intrinsic motivations is one of the five pillars of financial wellbeing.

The dark side is that a lack of dopamine can lead to depression. There is also the intense feeling of reward it can provide from taking addictive drugs.

This is also true of **serotonin**, which is sometimes called the 'leadership' chemical. This is because we get serotonin when we are admired or respected. It is also generated from exercise, as are all of these four chemicals, and from sunshine.

And then there is **oxytocin**, the 'chemical of love,' so called because it is released during physical and social contact, or when we fall in love. It also has a possible negative side, however – for example, it can explain why people mistrust outsiders.

If these are the chemicals that bring about happiness – the chemicals without which we may feel depressed – then our plan to use our money to accumulate life must take them into account. We need to keep reminding ourselves what our money is for.

Understanding what causes these chemicals to appear in our brains is like taking a shortcut to finding happiness. You can find more information about each of the chemicals, and what you can do to generate them, in *Appendix 2: How to Generate the Happy Chemicals*. Suffice it to say, a person who focuses their time on exercise, physical contact, being part of a community, eating well and being outdoors (i.e. the five elements of wellbeing in *Chapter 8*) will (all other things being equal) be more happy than a person who does not.

And this relationship goes both ways. For example, one study found that those people in a group with the highest level of positive thoughts were three times less likely to catch a cold than those with the lowest level of positive thoughts.[79]

These changes are so simple, and are things that we surely already know. You don't need to buy a book to tell you that eating well and exercising will make you happier. And yet we don't make these changes.

What prevents us from changing our behaviour? Fatalism may be one issue – acceptance of things the way they are, or the idea that things won't really change.

There is one area of scientific study that has seen huge strides over the past few decades that might just strike a blow to the fatalistic attitude. With the right training, we can change our brains.

NEUROPLASTICITY

Neuroscientists have been investigating the physical changes that take place in the brain as a result of life's experiences. The results show that certain parts of the brain become more active when we experience pleasure or joy, or when we are unhappy or depressed. Which leads to the question of whether these areas could be stimulated, just like we go to the gym to work on our bodies.

Scientists have realised that "through mental activity alone we can intentionally change our own brains."[80]

These results are hugely important for any study of happiness as they show that we *are* in control of our own brains! There are a number of techniques for changing the way your brain works, such as meditation. Studies have shown that Buddhist monks who are experts in a type of practice called 'love and kindness meditation' have more highly developed sections of the brain that relate to joy.[81]

If we introduce it to new thoughts or experiences, the brain creates new neural pathways. The more this new information or experience is reinforced, the greater the chance that these new neural pathways will wire together, with older, less used pathways being pruned to make way for the new. This is a process known as 'tuning and pruning.'[82]

When we add together all of the aspects of our brains and bodies that this book has discussed so far – happy chemicals in our brains, training the areas of the brain that bring wellbeing and the fact that overall wellbeing is great for our immune system – we can see that how we use our finances can have a huge impact on our health. And, best of all, it is all within our control.

This also puts the role of money in our lives in its proper context. Money is a tool that we can use to generate wellbeing. However, money can also be an *enemy* of wellbeing if accumulation of money becomes the objective of our plans.

TIP FOR FINANCIAL ADVISERS: Financial advisers can play a crucial role in introducing new ideas and suggestions, and these in turn can start the unseen process of the brain rewiring itself. Reinforce these enough, through this 'tuning and pruning' process, and biology will be on your side. The brain will create new neural pathways and therefore enhance the capabilities of the person with whom you are working.

MORE THEORIES OF HAPPINESS

Let's take a trip around some of the other theories about what makes us happy, to identify what else we can learn about our relationship with money.

COMPARISON IS THE THIEF OF JOY[83]
Comparison theory states that happiness comes from the perceived gap between the reality of our lives and common standards ('keeping up with the Joneses').

Who determines these standards? Well, society does, to a point – but so does the media.

Advertising, for example, specifically tries to show us how much cooler we might be if we bought the product – you know, the one everyone is talking about? The bestselling one, the one that is endorsed by that cool celebrity? This messaging attempts to place that product as the one that is the common standard for happiness, and invites us to compare ourselves to other people. Spending money on buying this product, so the intimation goes, will bring us wellbeing, just like the person in the advert.

> Many years ago a work friend had a terminally ill son. The teenage lad had already lived longer than had been predicted. When it was time for him to start senior school aged 11, my friend's family asked the head teacher if the school would accept their son. The head replied that it wasn't a case of accepting him – the school insisted he go there.
>
> The sixth-form students organised themselves into a rota so that one of them would be at the end of every class to help him get to his next lesson. The lad was on a lot of different drugs and, I believe, would have been in a lot of pain. Despite this, he was a joy to be around.
>
> My friend once asked his son how he managed to keep so cheerful. "Oh, that's easy, Dad," the teenager replied. "There are lots of people worse off than me."

Sixty years or more of psychological research into social comparisons tells us that we tend to evaluate ourselves by making comparisons to those who seem *better off* than we are – whether this is happier, wealthier or more 'successful.'[84]

This does not mean comparison theory's implications are always bad – you can make it work for you. Comparing upwards tends to make us unhappy, but comparing downwards can make us realise how lucky we are. This, however, is not what we tend to do.

If we can understand our own intrinsic motivations, we are less likely to look at others and feel envious. Your financial wellbeing plan should therefore help to reduce some of that comparison anxiety.

NEED THEORY

Happiness comes from whether certain needs are being gratified. Need theory suggests that the ability to be happy is within us but that we are unable to experience happiness until certain other basic requirements have been met, and in a particular order.

According to Maslow's hierarchy of needs, we first have our basic needs of food and shelter. Then we need to feel safe, for example to be healthy, or perhaps to have a decent job.[85]

Once we feel safe, we can focus on the need to belong – to be part of a family and/or community. Next comes self-esteem, perhaps a sense of purpose. It is at this level, Maslow argued, that happiness is able to flourish, and this allows us to reach the final level, a stage of self-actualisation.

As the name implies, this hierarchy suggests that you cannot move up to the next level until you have completed the level below. Maslow himself accepted that this is not accurate – for example it is possible to feel part of a community while not having enough to eat. Nevertheless, the model provides us with some clear rules, and they have found their way into the principles of financial planning.

For example, any financial adviser worth their salt will advise you to keep an amount of money in readily realisable form (i.e. cash) as an emergency fund. Ideally this will be an amount covering three to six months of your normal expenditure. If you don't have such a fund, putting away an amount each month to build up an emergency fund will provide peace of mind – and make moving up the hierarchy of needs easier.

The hierarchy teaches us one other important lesson about our relationship to money. The lower levels of need can be obtained and/or improved by money. Food and water, shelter, security of self and of health – in our modern world, money has a part to play in all these. As we move up the hierarchy, however, into friendship, love and self-actualisation (a form of meaning and purpose), money has less or no part to play. This provides a theoretical basis for the research (explored in *Chapter 8*) which showed that, after a certain point (said to be $95,000 per year), more money won't make you more happy.

At the self-esteem level of Maslow's hierarchy, it might seem that money can provide the respect of others. However, as we have seen from looking at internal and external self-worth, if this respect is due to external factors, such as being wealthy, then it can be taken away. Indeed, a focus on money might even block the way to the next level.

Self-esteem that derives from internal self-worth is more likely to allow us to reach the highest level of happiness: self-actualisation (characterised by Maslow as creativity, lack of prejudice and a stage of personal growth).

THE FINANCIAL
WELLBEING JUNKIE

Let's return now to the set point theory of wellbeing (introduced in *Chapter 6*) and consider this way of looking at happiness in a little more depth. What does this theory tell us about our love of spending money on buying things?

Hedonic adaptation is a psychological model that forms part of set point theory. We have established that our level of happiness tends not to change throughout our lives, and that around half of that level of happiness is inherited. When we have an experience that creates either positive or negative stimulation, this produces a gain or a loss in our short-term happiness. As the stimulus reduces and then disappears, so our wellbeing stabilises.

This means that after a positive (or negative) event that pushes us above (or below) our set level of happiness, we return to that set level.

Understanding this model provides a key to unlocking one of the secrets to happiness – that short-term fixes of happiness do not affect long-term wellbeing, and that we need to make much longer-term changes. It backs up our 'living a life with meaning and purpose' objective.

A layperson's term for 'hedonic adaptation' might be 'getting used to things.' Events, whether they create positive stimuli or negative, cease to have an effect as they become the new normal. In this way, we oscillate around that set point.

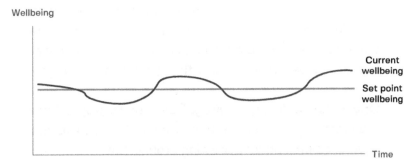

When we are above our set point, when we feel happy, there is no imperative to force us back down. When we are below the set point, feeling unhappy, we want to get back up to it as quickly as possible. And one way of achieving this is to buy stuff. There is even a name for this – retail therapy.

This continual spending of money in an attempt to raise our level of wellbeing through short-term fixes makes us all financial wellbeing junkies.

To escape this loop, we should use our money to generate wellbeing that has a longer-lasting effect. One example would be to buy experiences over luxury items, as they create longer-lasting wellbeing through memories. If these are with friends and loved ones, then we are also playing into the fact that social wellbeing is the strongest contributor to overall wellbeing.

When constructing a financial wellbeing plan, therefore, it is important to focus on things that will increase long-term wellbeing. As we saw in *Chapter 9*, bucket list items are important and can create a wellbeing 'tail' if they are based on your intrinsic motivations rather than short-term goals. Living with meaning and purpose, however, will have a much longer-term effect.

> I am a cricket fan, and went to see my beloved Gloucestershire County Cricket Club play one Sunday. The weather forecast wasn't great, and it did rain for several hours. I waited hopefully, but the game was called off.
>
> Driving home, feeling grumpy, I decided to stop off at a favourite record shop, Rough Trade in Bristol. I bought several albums on vinyl, costing around £50.
>
> As I drove home, I gave myself a slap on the forehead. I had, quite literally, just done what I tell others not to do! With my wellbeing nudged below my set point, I had sought a short-term hit of happiness by buying some records that I didn't need.

Exercise 11 in *Appendix 1: Your Financial Wellbeing Plan* may help you to ascertain how much of a financial wellbeing junkie you might be, and whether this is an issue you need to be concerned with.

CONSTRUCTING PERMANENT REMINDERS OF WHAT MAKES YOU HAPPY

Some researchers compare our set point level of wellbeing to inherited illnesses. Does this mean that we are destined to forever oscillate around a set level of wellbeing?[86]

One way to stop being financial wellbeing junkies is to put in place mechanisms to remind us of the things that make us happy. If we notice that certain things in our lives are gradually causing us less wellbeing, then we should remind ourselves of the value of those positive things and what life would be like without them.

The Greek philosopher Epictetus took this to an extreme level when he suggested that every time you kiss your child good night, you can imagine them dying the next day.[87] In this way, you will appreciate and get wellbeing from the ones you love by imagining them not being there. I'm not suggesting such an extreme approach, but hopefully the example gets across the principle!

Creating your own financial wellbeing plan can help you to keep track of these things that you value. Most importantly, the plan should be *added to* each year – document your progress by updating the status of each action rather than replacing actions. The aim is to create an audit trail over time of the actions you have taken to improve your wellbeing. In this way it can become a permanent reminder of the work you are putting in to improve your wellbeing.

TIP FOR FINANCIAL ADVISERS: Why not produce a financial wellbeing report that shows what the client has achieved and what makes them happy? Bring this to the client for every meeting, and perhaps open the meeting by going through the report. Reminding the client of of the positive steps they are taking will provide a continuous reminder and help to ensure that their financial planning continues to focus on their wellbeing.[88]

WELLBEING FROM GIVING

During his discussions about joy with the Dalai Lama, Archbishop Desmond Tutu said, "Joy is your reward for the giving of joy."[89] Spending your time – and some of your money – spreading joy is a great way to generate your own wellbeing. This is not just philanthropy – it is an attitude to life. If giving becomes a habit, it can have the long-term effect we are seeking.

When we turn this attitude towards our finances, we see that "giving is good for you"[90] – *as long as* you approach it in the right way, for example by giving in order to bring joy to others, not attention to yourself.

And yet the amount of charitable giving is pitifully small. In the UK an 'ultra-high-net-worth' person is defined as someone worth £10 million or more. In 2019, the average amount people in the UK in that wealth bracket gave to charity was *under £500*.[91] When you consider the enormous sums given to charity by a few wealthy people, this means that the vast majority of people who have more money than they will ever need give little or nothing to charity each year.

Leaving aside the moral aspect of this statistic, people who do not give – whether it is time or money – are missing out on a major source of wellbeing.

Financial advice professional Kim Bendall had helped a client in her late sixties, Sally, to realise that she was in the fortunate position of having more money than she needed. Kim's firm asked Sally what she would like to do with the excess money.

Sally's childhood had been by the sea. She had often sat on the harbour watching volunteer lifeboat crews going out to save lives. The result of the discussion was that Sally paid for a new lifeboat in a small fishing village in Ireland. She travelled over for the launch and made friends with the crew. She subsequently visited often, and loved taking the crew out to lunch.

In return the RNLI (Royal National Lifeboat Institution) made sure that Sally was kept informed of all relevant callouts, press clippings and so on. Often, when the lifeboat saved a life, the rescued person would write a message that was sent on to Sally.

This philanthropy not only brought Sally immeasurable wellbeing but also, Kim believed, added years to her life.[92]

When creating your giving plan, here are three simple rules to follow to maximise wellbeing:
- Plan your giving so it comes from a position of joy, not guilt
- Link your giving to your personal values
- See the impact of your giving (maybe even get involved)

Part of your financial wellbeing plan, therefore, should be to consider your giving. In constructing your philanthropy plan, remember than giving isn't just about money – it is also about time. As well as being great for your self-worth, it can also help you to connect with others, thereby increasing the community element of your wellbeing.

David was the managing director of a business. When David sold his shares, he spent time considering what he might do next. He still needed to work, but a serious accident had made him reflect on the life that he had been leading.

David decided to split his working week three ways. He would spend one day a week on community projects (as a governor at his children's school), one day on charity work (he joined a local charity as a trustee) and three days on business (he became a director of a local firm).

The word 'philanthropy' means "the disposition or active effort to promote the happiness and wellbeing of others."[93] In this way it is different to 'giving.' It means putting some thought into what you are giving and to whom you are giving it. See Exercise 12 in *Appendix 1: Your Financial Wellbeing Plan*, on how to build your own philanthropy plan.

TIP FOR FINANCIAL ADVISERS: At the Institute for Financial Wellbeing conference in 2020, philanthropy expert Emma Beeston explained that, at least in the UK, people are embarrassed to bring up the subject of philanthropy, and would like their advisers to raise it with them. As advisers very rarely bring the subject up themselves, philanthropy does not get discussed in the financial planning process and giving remains incredibly low.

Given the wellbeing that can be had from philanthropy, a financial-wellbeing-oriented adviser will make sure that giving is on the agenda with clients. You may decide to offer to help clients prepare a philanthropy plan, using some of the principles outlined in this book.[94]

DELAYED CONSUMPTION

We live in an age not just of consumerism but of *instant* consumerism. Films, games, music – we have instant access to entertainment via our phones or by streaming on the TV. We are now accustomed to next-day delivery. In the process, we have lost the enjoyment of anticipation.[95]

Try this exercise. Think of something that you once looked forward to – perhaps something you needed to save up for. Try and remember the feeling of excitement and anticipation leading up to the buying of the thing. Now try to remember your level of enjoyment once you owned the item. Compare one with the other.

There is wellbeing to be had from anticipation. We have already looked at the importance of buying experiences, not stuff. This is because experiences create memories. There is the excitement from looking forward to creating those memories.

A study looked at around 1,500 people, some of whom were going on holiday and some whom were not. Those going on holiday reported greater happiness before the trip than those who weren't, yet both reported the same level of happiness after the travellers returned from their trip.[96]

And yet, of course, those who had the holiday will *also* be able to look at the pictures and relive the memories for years to come.

Another example is Christmas. The build-up to Christmas can take weeks, even months. And yet Christmas itself is often over in a flash. It is the anticipation of Christmas, and the excitement of giving and getting presents, that brings so much excitement.

> A friend told me their experience of ordering a new car, which showed how the car manufacturer used anticipation to generate brand loyalty. Once the order had been placed, the owner-to-be began receiving correspondence – from the car!
>
> First an email would arrive where the car introduced itself. This was followed by updates about how it was being built. A mug with a picture of the car arrived in the post. More messages arrived, all designed to create a relationship with the purchase far beyond owning a physical object. As my friend told me, "Once the car actually turned up, I didn't know whether to drive it or make love to it!"

As we have seen from the discussions of the 'fight-or-flight' response in *Part One*, we are programmed to want our gratification now. But if there is a significant purchase you are keen to make – take your time over it. If you have a holiday planned, take time in the weeks and months leading up to it to think about it – perhaps plan excursions or think about what book you are going to read by the pool. There is an exercise relating to this in *Appendix 1: Your Financial Wellbeing Plan* (see Exercise 13).

Here's a tip that really goes against modern living – pay for everything in cash. Take out an amount that you have budgeted to spend in cash at the beginning of the month. When it's gone, it's gone.

And, if it is possible for you, consider getting rid of the credit card. Credit cards offer the opposite of pleasure from delaying consumption – they encourage consuming now and paying later. There have been lots of studies that show how credit cards encourage not only more spending, but reckless spending.

In one study, researchers auctioned off baseball tickets to business students. One group were told to pay by cash, the other group by credit card. The average cash bid was $28 whereas the average credit card bid was $60.[97]

Another study asked people to estimate their credit card bill. Every single person underestimated the bill, and by an average of 30%.[98]

Credit cards encourage you to *consume now, pay later*. A better approach for healthier finances is to *pay now, consume later*. It's better for budgeting, *and* it brings with it wellbeing from delaying consumption.

CONCLUSION

We have now considered two of our four cornerstones of financial wellbeing, the 'wellbeing' row of our model. We have looked at what brings wellbeing to all of us, in terms of how to live a life with meaning and purpose, and we have considered some practicalities around our money habits. We have looked at how to 'know thyself' – to learn what will bring each of us wellbeing in our own way.

Now we will consider what might be working *against* us: the aspects of our relationship to money that lead us to make poor financial decisions. We will again take the approach of looking at these barriers to wellbeing in terms of the behavioural biases that are the same for all of us, before looking at our individual beliefs.

● ● ● ●

CHAPTER 11

HOW YOUR BEHAVIOURS INFLUENCE YOUR FINANCIAL OUTCOMES

We have focused on the positive steps we can take to achieve a better relationship with money, and thereby increase our financial wellbeing. We have established that we make financial decisions with System 1 – gut feelings, emotional decisions. Slowing down the financial decision-making process will make it easier to make money-related decisions with System 2. We've searched for our own intrinsic motivations, in order to create a clear path to living a life with meaning and purpose.

We have looked at the factors that *create wellbeing* that are *common to all of us*.

We have sought to 'know thyself,' to understand what *creates wellbeing* that is *individual to each of us*.

In this and the next chapter, we are going to look at what might derail these plans, starting with *barriers to wellbeing* that are common to all of us – the behaviours and biases that affect how we make financial decisions.[99]

Note: these chapters only touch the surface of the field of behavioural economics. We are seeking to highlight some of the main biases that affect our financial decisions so as to help to create – and deliver – your financial wellbeing plan. If you find this field interesting, there are many books that are available solely on this subject.[100]

BEHAVIOURAL
FINANCE OVERVIEW

Behavioural economics has developed enormously over the past few decades. From the 1970s, economists began to realise that their economic models of how capitalism operates made many sweeping assumptions about how people behave.

'All other things being equal' is one of the most common expressions you hear in economics. One of the most fundamental assumptions is that everyone behaves in certain ways.

I studied economics at university. At the start of the second year, we had a lecture on indifference curves, an economic model that describes how consumers value two different products. For this introductory lecture, the professor had chosen beer and wine as the two products.

Halfway through the talk, a student put up their hand. "But sir," they said, "I drink cider." Cue chuckles from the students.

"Very funny," said the lecturer. "For now, let's assume that everyone drinks either beer or wine." He tried to continue the lecture.

"But sir," interrupted the student. "I really do drink cider. How do I fit into this model?"

The lecturer put down the piece of chalk he had been writing with (I am *that* old) and turned to face the class. "Let's get something straight," he said. "Both you and I know that this has no bearing on what happens in the real world. But that won't help you pass the course. So just write down what I say so you can repeat it in the exam.

Behavioural finance is a subset of behavioural economics and has become a very popular topic. It describes the study of human behaviours, specifically around money.

We all exhibit behavioural biases, all the time. Many of these are good for us, having been fine-tuned through our evolutionary development to protect us from harm, either physical or mental. Some, however, get in the way of making good decisions. This is especially true when the decision involves emotions, as is the case with financial decisions.

How we behave in certain circumstances can be predicted, and it often isn't in our own best interests. And even our predictable behaviours can be used against us, for example in advertising.

Behavioural finance has become big business. Consultancy firms have been set up on how to use behavioural knowledge to sell more of their clients' products. To me, that's rather like buying a piano in order to use it for firewood.

Books have been written on how to use behavioural finance knowledge to "beat the investment markets." That to me feels like a travel journalist writing an article titled "The Ten Best Unspoilt Beauty Spots."

In this and the next chapter, we will dip our toes in the water of behavioural finance in an attempt to remove some of the blockages to living a life with meaning and purpose. We will be interested in learning about what biases we might unknowingly exhibit which prevent us from making good financial decisions.

Let's begin by looking at a bias that actually gets in the way of learning.

THE DUNNING–KRUGER EFFECT

David Dunning and Justin Kruger developed a theory about how we learn new information and how we assess our own competency.[101] In simple terms, it says that you need to be reasonably intelligent to understand how stupid you are.

As with so many biases, there is an old expression that is a good shortcut to understanding the Dunning–Kruger effect: "A little knowledge is a dangerous thing."[102] As we learn something new, we tend to reach a point where think we have gained understanding. If we just learned a little more about the topic, however, we would start to realise that we don't really understand the topic at all, and there is much more on the subject we don't know.

Some people suffer from this bias more than others. Its presence will be seen when someone overestimates their abilities. One example would be someone who makes an investment in the stock market just at the time when the markets are generally going upwards. They think investing is something they clearly have a talent for, only to find out when the markets go down that maybe they didn't have 'the secret' after all!

Do-it-yourself investors, therefore, who feel that they do not need to employ a financial adviser because they already know enough themselves, should ensure that they continue to learn and research.

We should all beware (and be aware of) the Dunning–Kruger effect. It affects everyone and leads to complacency. If you 'think' you're really good at something but you're not, then poor outcomes are almost inevitable.

The solution, as with many of the biases, lies in slowing down and trying to use System 2 when making decisions. A quick decision is likely to use System 1, and this may mean not taking into account all the information available.

Simply knowing that the Dunning–Kruger effect exists should help you. Whenever you feel that you understand something fully, seek out more information or talk to experts. You may well find there is more to know!

TIP FOR FINANCIAL ADVISERS: There has become a trend in recent years for financial advisers to use behavioural finance to manage clients when they are behaving in a way that we would consider to be bad.

To do so, however, requires a judgement on what is 'bad.' There is a danger that such a judgement will be based upon the adviser's values, not the client's.

For example, suppose a client is invested in the stock market, which goes down. The client wants to cash in. Selling at the bottom is clearly not a good thing to do, and we can point to various biases, such as loss aversion, that are coming into play. The adviser tells the client to stay invested.

The market then goes down a little further, causing this client huge distress and discomfort. It might not be the right thing to exit the stock market because it's gone down, but if the values and beliefs of this client are so strong that it will negatively impact their wellbeing, then to go against this may make them unhappy. There are times when we have to respect their wishes, to allow them to make the 'wrong' decision.

Educate, of course; point out the behavioural biases driving their behaviour, absolutely; question whether they should be invested in the first place, maybe. Ultimately, however, the role of the adviser is to construct a financial plan that is in accordance with the client's own values and beliefs, and not those of the adviser. We are not there to manage clients' behaviour but to educate and guide them.

The Dunning–Kruger effect is even relevant to readers of this book! If you've reached this far in the book and are still reading, you may well have a low level of this bias.

CONFIRMATION BIAS

This behavioural bias describes our tendency to seek out information that confirms our existing views. A person with certain political beliefs is likely to buy a daily newspaper that reflects (and therefore confirms) those beliefs, rather than a newspaper that might challenge them. They will follow people on social media who think like them.

A person with strong confirmation bias is going to struggle to see things in a different way than they already do – and that includes about their own lives. This might make it hard to picture their future self and to create a meaningful financial plan.

> Colin and Joanna were conflicted. They had a daughter wanting to set up a business as a personal trainer. Their son had recently married. He and his wife had their first child on the way, and they wanted to buy a house. Joanna wanted to help out their kids, but Colin thought they needed to keep hold of their money for their own financial security. Colin had previously exhibited a strong confirmation bias.
>
> In a meeting with their financial planner, Joanna had asked Colin, "Why do we need so much money?" In response, Colin listed a number of reasons – all based on his existing beliefs. The challenge-type question had made Colin defensive and thus played into Colin's confirmation bias.
>
> The financial planner then asked the question, "What is the purpose of your money?" By linking the money to Colin and Joanna's intrinsic motivations of caring for their children, the financial planner helped the discussion to move in a more positive direction.

Is this you? Do you dismiss new information? Do you quickly form views without evidence? Do you seek back-up of your views from others? You might ask these questions of those who know you well – if you find yourself dismissing their honest answers, this might well confirm your tendency to confirmation bias!

The first tip if you think this might describe you is to recognise that you might need help from a third party, whether this is a friend, a financial coach or a financial planner. It is very difficult to challenge our own assumptions, and this is especially the case for those with strong confirmation bias.

TIP FOR FINANCIAL ADVISERS: If you think a client exhibits strong confirmation bias, keep your questions simple and neutral. It is very easy to ask a question that allows a client to confirm what they are already thinking.

An important ongoing tip is to provide evidence for a client with strong confirmation bias, in order to augment their flow of information from just that which confirms their existing view. Why not make a specific note on their file, so that everyone in the firm understands how this person makes decisions?

FRAMING

Framing is a bias that is present in everyone. It relates to how information is presented. For example, if we describe the results of a survey as "80% of customers were satisfied," this sounds a lot better than "20% of customers were unsatisfied"!

> Framing is used all the time in parenting. If my parents wanted my brother and me to get ready for bed, I would make a fuss. My father would then take out his watch and tell us he would time us on how long it took to get our pyjamas on. Now it was a competition against my brother, and we would fly up the stairs. Worked every time!

Framing can be used to manage expectations. If you have a meeting with a solicitor, they will very often have ranks of old leather books in a bookcase at the side of the meeting room. Do they ever take out one of the dusty volumes to look up an ancient ruling that might turn the tide of your case? Of course not.

> **TIP FOR FINANCIAL ADVISERS:** When a client visits a financial adviser, they are expecting to get advice about their finances, especially if it is their first time. As we are seeing throughout this book, however, the financial advice process starts with helping a client to work out what a life with meaning and purpose might mean for them.
>
> Popular questions in recent years have been variants of "What does money mean to you?" Intended to steer the client away from a conversation about their pension

and investments, the question actually frames the conversation to be entirely about money!

Framing can be used to prepare clients for a conversation about intrinsic motivations that they might not normally expect from a financial adviser. Your newsletter, blog and articles, social media activity, the email confirming the appointment – all of these can be used to ensure that the client is open to a conversation that, at least initially, isn't about money.

Framing will influence your decisions in ways that you do not intend. Suppose you and your partner are thinking about what you might do when the children leave home. A natural question might be "Will you play more golf?" (at least for someone who plays golf!). However, this frames retirement to be about golf. Instead, you might ask, "Is there anything you haven't done that you would like to?" Or perhaps a simple "What might retirement mean to you?"

We often frame our future around what we think we can afford. This places our future in the context of preconceived ideas about money. And yet you now know from all that you have read so far in this book that, after a certain (and fairly low) point, more money doesn't make you more happy. We should therefore frame any discussion about our future to be about our wellbeing, not about money.

HERDING

There is comfort to be found in following the lead of others. This is the basic concept behind celebrity endorsements – if someone famous says a product is worth buying, then it must be! Even the briefest analysis of whether there is sound logic behind this assumption shows how daft it is, and yet it works.

We have a tendency to take actions based on what we see others are doing. This can be seen often in the stock market, where downward movement often triggers people to sell, and a long upward run creates the confidence to buy.

We tend to make financial decisions based on what other people think. For example, we will often ask for the opinions of our friends and family, or of our professional advisers. There is a danger, however, that we will then make a decision that is based on their values, not our own.

In my early days as a financial planner, a client came in for their first meeting. As all financial advisers are required to do, I asked the client what he felt about investment risk. Where might he put himself on a scale of one, meaning a low appetite for risk, to five, high?

He thought momentarily, then replied, "I'm not sure. What does everyone else say?"

In order to avoid any herding bias, as you complete your financial wellbeing plan, continually ask yourself the following question: "How well aligned is this decision with my intrinsic motivations and my values?" It is key that the plan is one that is right for *you*, not based on what other people think.

LOSS AVERSION

Nobody likes to lose something, so loss aversion is present in everyone. Think about what it is like to lose something, or how you feel when you open a pension statement and your investments have gone down in value. Now try and imagine the feeling when you find the item you thought you had lost, or you see your investments have gone up in value.[103]

As mentioned in *Chapter 8*, we feel a loss on average 3.69 times more than we feel an equivalent gain. This is why the objective of financial planning must be *achievable* intrinsic motivations. *Not* achieving your motivations will have a negative effect on your wellbeing – of a disproportionate amount than if you *did* achieve them.

It is also a reason why your financial wellbeing plan must focus on meaning and purpose, and not your savings and investments. One thing we know for certainty about investments is that at some point, they will go down. We are focused here on financial planning, with investment management being the 'engine' under the bonnet. Peeking under that bonnet is only going to lead to either a false sense of joy or a (disproportionately larger) sense of disappointment.

PRESENT BIAS

We have already looked at our tendency to focus on immediate gratification rather than delayed gratification, to make financial decisions based on 'fight or flight.' We all have a degree of present bias, as we find it difficult to picture our future self. For some it is even harder than for others.

Given two identical prizes, we are more likely to choose one that we get now than one we will get after a delay.[104] We all differ in how much we need to be tempted in order to persuade us to delay the prize. Perhaps I offered you £50 now or £60 in a week's time. Which would you take? What about £50 now or £80 in a week's time? And so on (another term for this is 'hyperbolic discounting').

Sometimes we can make present bias worse by making goals and targets too big, almost unachievable. So let's use different language. Dial down the pressure. Rather than talking about 'financial freedom' (a common term in some sectors), just think in terms of having options. Don't talk about retirement, but instead think of spending your time working at something you love.

Your financial plan is not set in stone. A phrase used by Greg Davies on *The Financial Wellbeing Podcast* works: "Keep the future just a little bit fuzzy."[105] In this way, the future might not seem so scary, and your bias towards the present may relax a little.

Cashflow forecasting from a financial planner is especially useful here. It enables you to see the effect of making various financial decisions on achieving future objectives. You can then weigh up the outcome against your plan on how to use your money today. By doing this you are actually using the universal bias of loss aversion in your favour!

> **TIP FOR FINANCIAL ADVISERS:** One key to overcoming our present bias is to make the future seem real. Firstly, you should make sure you have spent time helping a client to understand the real purpose of their financial plan, their achievable intrinsic motivations. You can then create that clear path using cashflow.
>
> By taking these steps, you are creating an image of the future. Now, whenever you talk about their savings and pensions, talk about "bringing the future closer." Make it seem real to the client.

ENDOWMENT EFFECT

We tend to value something we own more than someone else might value it. To put it another way, we demand a higher price when selling an item than we would be willing to pay if we bought the item. This is known as the 'endowment effect.'[106]

In the search for intrinsic motivations, people will tend to limit themselves to thinking about what they already have. In addition, people tend to see money as something that they 'own.' They may find decision-making difficult if it involves changes to their money if they have pronounced tendency to be influenced by the endowment effect.

This is one of the hardest biases to overcome. You need to dream about what might be, but cannot get past what already is. The phrase 'dare to dream' is one way of encouraging a person to think of things beyond what they already have. Check out Exercise 14 in *Appendix 1: Your Financial Wellbeing Plan* for some questions that might help here.

TIP FOR FINANCIAL ADVISERS: The use of silence can be especially helpful for people who are strongly influenced by the endowment effect – in other words, people who seem to be overvaluing their existing plans even when those plans do not fit with their newly discovered motivations.

For example, ask the question "Is there anything else you would like to do in retirement?" The client may immediately respond "No." Keep quiet and wait for them to speak next, no matter how long it takes. Their next answer is more likely to use System 2 thinking and may well elicit a deeper response.

MENTAL ACCOUNTING

When it comes to money, we tend to view the same amount very differently depending on the context. For example, if you have worked all day weeding someone's garden and received, say, £50 as payment, then you might put that money aside for something special. If, on the other hand, you found a £50 note on the street, you might feel it's 'extra' and spend it on a treat. And yet it's still £50 in each case.

Mental accounting can be a very positive behavioural bias for financial planning – in a way, it is a chance to provide financial wellbeing from anticipation. As a bias which can be very visual, people with high ability to use mental accounting can use images and names for certain pots of money to make them seem more real – to make the future seem more real.

TIP FOR FINANCIAL ADVISERS: You can use mental accounting to help clients stay focused on their financial plan and not get distracted. For example, if a client has a particular motivation in mind, use this to inspire them.

Perhaps they want to open a coffee shop, but only when their investment pot or pension reaches a certain amount. When you prepare for their annual review, include a picture of a coffee shop on the front of the review report.

Our mental accounting bias provides a great opportunity for visualisation opportunities. Here are some ideas for how to make your money seem more real:

- Use an image of a bank vault for a savings pot that has a particular time horizon, perhaps adding the date when it can be opened
- Use countdown reminders
- Give pots of money names (e.g. a certain bank account set aside for a dream holiday might be called the 'Machu Picchu Pot')
- Avoid anything that separates the payment from the thing that you are purchasing, unless it has been carefully budgeted for (so payment for a future holiday, great; paying by credit card, not so good)

There are plenty of apps that use mental accounting to help you to save.

But beware of this caveat: there can be a danger, when using images, of trying to fix your future. This can be stressful, especially if circumstances change. Mental accounting is therefore probably best used for modest financial goals.

CONCLUSION

Our behavioural biases are part of who we are. To be human means to be biased, which means that an attempt to fix or cure our biases is somewhat of a fool's errand. However, being aware that they exist, and understanding what triggers a bias in the first place, allows us to put in place strategies that can reduce any negative impact on the financial decision-making process.

Some of our behaviours are learned through experience. In this way, they have a lot in common with the last of our four areas of financial wellbeing and the second area that addresses barriers to making good financial decisions: our financial beliefs.

CHAPTER 12

●●●●

YOUR
FINANCIAL
BELIEFS

To recap: we have looked at the factors that *create wellbeing* that are *common to all of us.*

We have sought to 'know thyself' – to understand what *creates wellbeing* that is *individual to each of us.*

We have looked at *barriers to wellbeing* that are *common to all of us.*

To complete our financial wellbeing plan, we need to understand the *barriers to wellbeing* that are *individual to each of us.*

In this chapter we will look at the extent to which our own attitudes and actions may be resulting in poor financial outcomes. We need to consider how they might prevent us from realising our financial wellbeing plan, and what we might do about this. We will also look at the money diversions that contribute to those attitudes, with the result that we build barriers against creating a relationship with money that is focused on wellbeing.

It might feel that some of these aspirations are out of our control. In fact, many, if not all of them, are up to us, if we choose to make it so. When we looked at the set point of wellbeing in *Chapter 6,* we learned that 40% of our wellbeing comes from our attitude, from our "intentional activity."[107] This is what makes these barriers individual to each of us, as we can choose how we respond to them. In this chapter, we need to adopt the approach that change is one of our options.

Some of these barriers are even *created* by us. Some of our behaviours are inherited, but many of them are driven by our beliefs. Not all of our beliefs, however, work in our own best interests.

SELF-LIMITING BELIEFS

We have looked at the importance of laying a firm foundation for *your* happiness. We want to build a financial wellbeing plan that is right for you, that will make *you* happy. The theories and principles that we have looked at have built a foundation, and these theories and principles should now include some of your intrinsic motivations.

You do, however, already *have* a foundation. These are the beliefs that you have built up throughout your life. The question we need to address is this: is your financial belief system providing the best bedrock for your wellbeing?

HOW BELIEFS DEVELOP

As we go through life, we have experiences. These experiences provide information. If I do X, then Y will happen. We might accept this as given (you don't trap your fingers in a car door more than once). Often, however, we will test whether this information is consistent by taking a similar action and seeing if we get a similar response.[108]

These actions might lead to new experiences that confirm the previous outcomes. Or they might create new outcomes. In time, the effect of this testing will be to modify our understanding of the world until the outcomes start to become solid – they become beliefs.

It is this set of beliefs that makes each of us unique. This is because they are beliefs based on the conclusions that we have drawn from a set of experiences that only *we* have lived.

This is why we are all different; we have all had different experiences, and we lead different lives.

People who have similar experiences will develop similar beliefs. This is what leads to culture. France, for example, has a culture of rebellion against authority. If you grow up in such a culture and you see that such rebellion often creates positive outcomes, you are more likely to be a rebellious person. Hence the French culture.

The same goes for our foundation blocks when we think about money. My parents' generation – the so-called baby boomers – grew up after the Second World War, when money was scarce. As a result, they tend to be hoarders and often find it difficult to spend money, especially on their own wellbeing. This pattern of behaviour means that many of them have developed a belief that they need more money to be secure than they actually do.

Maybe you have heard someone declare "I'm not very good with money." This isn't something that is true – it is a belief they might have reached because of habits that formed from their experiences. It is also a belief that is likely to result in poor financial decisions. As such, it is a 'self-limiting belief.'

What this adds up to is one of the important pieces of bedrock on which you will build your financial wellbeing plan:

Beliefs are not truths.

RECOGNISING YOUR SELF-LIMITING MONEY BELIEFS

Just because you believe something to be true does not necessarily mean that it is. When it comes to your beliefs about money, this is a concept that is worth spending some time with.

The fact that our beliefs are not truths does *not* mean that they are a problem. If we all thought the same way, if we all agreed on everything, the world would be a very dull place indeed! My friend who believes that 'insurance is a waste of time' has saved a lot of money on insurance premiums over the years. So far, this has not turned out to be a self-limiting belief – he hasn't lost wellbeing from not taking out insurance, as he would have been too irritated by what he sees as a waste of money. He would, of course, have felt very differently if his house had burnt down!

We are not, therefore, undertaking a root-and-branch overhaul of our beliefs. We are looking to spot beliefs we might have that are preventing us from achieving our financial wellbeing plan. Some examples of these might be:

- I'm not clever with money
- I must be bad with money because I have debt
- Money doesn't grow on trees
- Wanting more money makes me a bad person
- I don't deserve this money
- I should only spend money on others
- Investing is not for me
- Money makes you happy
- Money doesn't make you happy

Any of these beliefs could lead to poor financial outcomes and reduce the chances of you realising your financial wellbeing plan. You may now wish to complete part 1 of Exercise 15, on self-limiting beliefs, in *Appendix 1: Your Financial Wellbeing Plan.*

Michael was 16 years old when he spent a week's work experience at my then company, Ovation Finance Ltd. He was shown many aspects of the company's work, including researching client financial position, investment management, how to speak to clients and so on.

Towards the end of the week, I was asked to sit with him and explain the financial wellbeing principles upon which

Ovation was built. At one point I described the process of how people develop self-limiting beliefs.

Michael glanced at his phone to see if he had any messages. I noticed that the screen was smashed. I asked him how this had happened.

"I dropped it," he said. Looking slightly embarrassed, he elaborated, "Well, actually I threw it on the ground."

"What made you do that?" I asked.

"I told my friend that it was indestructible, and he bet me that it wasn't."

"What made you think your phone was indestructible?"

"Well, I had dropped it five times already, and it hadn't smashed. I therefore thought that it was indestructible. But my friend bet me that it wasn't, so I threw it on the ground. And it smashed."

I couldn't help but laugh. "You have quite literally just given the perfect description of how a self-limiting belief develops!"

PROBABILITY NEGLECT

We can return to the world of behavioural biases for a moment to shed a little light on how self-limiting beliefs arise. This might help us to unravel those beliefs that lead to poor financial decision-making.

Probability neglect is when we ignore the probability of something happening when making a decision.

Worldwide, about 24 people die each year from being hit by a champagne cork. There is an average of seven deaths each year from spiders.[109] And yet we are far more afraid of spiders than we are of champagne!

A person with high probability neglect may avoid investing in the stock market because they are afraid of losing all their money, even though the probably of this happening is virtually zero. Those baby boomers who believe that their money is going to run out, even when presented with evidence that it will not (such as a cashflow forecast), are doing a similar thing.

Do you have a worry or fear that you think might be irrational? The first step is to recognise and acknowledge this behaviour. You would not be alone in being concerned about the risks associated with the stock market, for example. Acknowledge what a big issue this is for you.

The question to ask yourself is whether a belief you hold is stopping you from achieving what you want to achieve. Is this a *self-limiting* belief? Being scared of spiders may be irrational, but it doesn't tend to impact our lives.

If this belief *is* self-limiting (and this may well be a difficult conclusion to admit to), you may then wish to take some time to think about how this belief might be changed.

CHANGING SELF-LIMITING BELIEFS

Now that we have established the principle that what we believe is not necessarily true, we open ourselves up to the possibility of any self-limiting beliefs being challenged. This may be key in preparing our financial wellbeing plan.

If experiences create beliefs, then it should be possible to reverse the process. To consider a belief, look at where it came from and then consider what alternative belief could have arrived instead.

We use our past as an anchor. "I do this because I've always done it. Because I've always done it, it's who I am. Because it's who I am, I do it again."

But what if it's not actually 'who you are'? What if you are only doing it because you've always done it? What if you are actually somebody different, you just don't know it because you're so busy being that other person? If it is making you unhappy, if it is creating poor financial decisions, then maybe it's time to replace that self-limiting belief with a different belief.

When it comes to changing our behaviours, there is an additional component: being open to accepting change.

Without the ability to accept that change is at least an option, all the understanding in the world will count for naught. A joke illustrates this. Question: How many financial coaches does it take to change a lightbulb? Answer: Only one, but the lightbulb has really got to want to change.

Some people try to avoid change. Trying to cling to something that is changing or has changed is likely to lead to unhappiness.[110] This is another reason why we need to use System 2 thinking when we are creating our plan and making financial decisions. Slow down, take time, deal with the challenge one step at a time. To quote the old expression, How do you eat an elephant? One mouthful at a time.

You may now wish to complete part 2 of Exercise 15, on self-limiting beliefs, in *Appendix 1: Your Financial Wellbeing Plan.*

NO 'MORE'

The notion of acceptance can be key when changing our attitudes and behaviours around money. We have seen that more money does not necessarily bring about more happiness. Yet our very economic system is based on us wanting 'more.' If you do not accept where you are, if you constantly strive for more, then you can never be satisfied with what you have.

This concept of acceptance is a tricky one, however. As a teenager, I had to finally accept that I was not going to play cricket for England. And yet how many people achieve sporting glory because they refused to accept that they would not succeed? (Note: such self-belief would not have made any difference in my chances of playing cricket for England for one simple reason – a lack of ability!)

Acceptance is something that allows us to have a *more sober* and *less emotional* reaction to events. It is about accepting the reality of the situation, rather than accepting that this is the *only* way it needs to be, or accepting the travails of life before deciding how best to react to them.

Archbishop Desmond Tutu spoke of an acceptance of reality as the place from which change can begin. He campaigned – successfully – for change to the apartheid system in South Africa, but this was only possible because "he did not accept the inevitability of apartheid, but he did accept its reality."[111]

Clinging to something that has changed may be an example of a self-limiting belief. Acceptance is a solution to this – acceptance of the reality, but an acceptance that is not conditional on whether that reality is right or good.[112]

ACCEPTANCE AND AMBITION

There is a paradox about the idea of acceptance that I'd like to address before moving on: how it impacts on ambition. I believe unlocking this might just make the difference, for some, in being able to take a step forward.

Many of the great inventions only come about because of people not accepting the way things currently work. Many an innovation or new business comes about because someone refuses to except the existing limitations. Ambition and hope sit at the heart of the extraordinary advances of humankind over the past few centuries.

Does this mean that inventors and entrepreneurs are unhappy people? Does a constant striving for change mean that happiness is not available to you?

I was discussing this conundrum of acceptance and ambition with a friend, Colin Low, who is also a financial planner and a member of the Institute for Financial Wellbeing. Colin has a deep-seated Christian faith, which helps to give him a perspective on such issues.

Colin said that he saw the two concepts in different frames. Acceptance, he felt, was a macro issue, something that relates to his life. He could accept what he was taught about God, what Jesus taught, and could accept the limitations that life had given him as well as the opportunities.

His ambition, however, existed in smaller steps. He didn't accept that financial planners could only work in one way, which was why he set up his own company. In this way, acceptance gave him a grounding in life, but ambition and hope also enabled him to find contentment that was appropriate to him.

The solution to the paradox of acceptance and ambition comes from accepting reality without judgement. It is possible to accept that things are as they are, but still strive for change to improve how they might be. Indeed, acceptance of our current situation enables us to better identify the best course of action.

In this way, we can change our perspective from clinging to something that has changed, which may well be a self-limiting belief, and instead accept the reality of that change.

PERMISSION

We spend so much time thinking of others that we often forget to think of ourselves. We follow patterns of behaviour, and then expect others and ourselves to conform to that pattern – even if it is not helpful or what we really want to do. The words 'should' and 'shouldn't' are often used when we make decisions.[113]

Giving yourself permission in relation to money doesn't mean permission to treat yourself to things you don't need. In the context of financial wellbeing, it means giving yourself permission to live a life with meaning and purpose. Giving yourself permission to be happy.

> As a business owner, husband, son, parent and friend, I used to spend a lot of my time worrying about whether other people had the right circumstances in order to be happy.
>
> At the same time, I became depressed, as diagnosed by my GP. I sought help from business coaching, and realised that I was not doing one particular thing that gave me joy – writing novels.

I wanted to go to a four-day week at my company, Ovation Finance, and use the 'free' day to write creatively. I was worried, however, about what impact the boss taking a day a week out might have on the morale of the Ovation team.

I spoke privately to one of them, Vickie. I asked her what she thought the reaction might be in the office to me moving to a four-day week.

"We're all part time," she replied. "Why shouldn't you be?"

I realised that she was right – every single employee had flexibility around their time except me! Vickie's reply was revelatory to me – I needed the permission of the team to feel that I could do something for me. I still take Wednesdays to write and have so far published three novels.

The issue of permission may be one of your blockages to creating your financial wellbeing plan.

Sometimes we compare ourselves with others in order to justify what *we* would like to do. In the example of my moving to a four-day week, it was not just about Vickie giving me permission – it was the realisation that the change I wanted to make was only bringing me in line with everyone else.

This can also work against us if we do *not* allow ourselves to do something that others *don't* do. We tend to gravitate to the familiar, even if it is not in our best interests. We might therefore look to others and decide that if they don't have something, maybe we shouldn't have it either. This is known as 'comparative suffering.'

Permission affects many aspects of our lives. Permission to fail, for example, by recognising that failing at something doesn't mean to others what it might mean to us.[114] Permission to be creative, or to do a job that you enjoy but that doesn't pay as well.

A lack of any or all of these may be preventing you from giving yourself permission to be happy. It takes courage to be different, to make decisions only based on your wellbeing. Yet this is key – your first step must be to give yourself permission to change. Hope is not a strategy![115]

That step might be easier to take if the change in question seems feasible – and this is where your financial wellbeing plan comes in. As we have already seen, living a life with meaning and purpose invariably involves helping others in some way. If you follow the principles of this book – that happiness comes from self-worth, which comes from compassion and being kind to others – then working through this book might help you to give yourself permission to be happy.

You may also use a third party to help you test the impact of the change. This might be a coach, or a financial planner with coaching training. For example, a change of career to one that brings you greater fulfilment but lower earnings might seem selfish. Financial planning may demonstrate that it is not actually selfish, because you can afford to do it.

Ultimately, the permission to be happy must come from within.[116] You might now work through Exercise 16, on permission, in *Appendix 1: Your Financial Wellbeing Plan.*

MONEY DISTRACTIONS

These concepts of change, acceptance and permission, indeed the very challenge of adopting a attitude to money based on wellbeing not accumulation, are especially tough to overcome because there are so many distractions working against us – outside influences that tempt us away from using money to accumulate life.

We have previously looked at the idea of success, and how society, through the media and advertising, tends to equate success with money. Now let's take a stroll around some of the other preconceptions in our relationship with money, and look at them in light of what we now know about the causes of happiness.

TIP FOR FINANCIAL ADVISERS: What follow are more reasons why you need to be proactive in your conversations with clients about their financial wellbeing.

We are conditioned to see accumulation of wealth and assets as being sources of happiness. There are many vested interests promoting consumerism, and yet we have seen that this reduces wellbeing, especially if we buy stuff we don't need, which prevents us from achieving intrinsic motivations.

If you provide cashflow forecasting with clients, it is likely that you have some information about their spending. Ask yourself: Is their spending helping them to achieve wellbeing? Or are their spending habits working against their wellbeing? To what extent are they influenced by external factors or self-limiting beliefs?

As we run through some of these money distractions, ask yourself this question: Are any of these external factors affecting *my* financial wellbeing? Are they influencing your financial decisions away from your intrinsic motivations?

ADVERTISING

One objective of advertising is to make you feel unhappy while simultaneously providing the solution. The beer advert that suggests you will jump the queue if you drink that beer. The product that suggests you will only be beautiful and cool if you look like a model or actor (any perfume advert). I could go on and on, but you get the point.

Remember the financial wellbeing junkie from *Chapter 10*? Adverts are there to encourage that habit. A focus on what you *have* leads to wellbeing. But advertising insists that you focus on what you *don't have*. Turn off the adverts. Mute or avoid them whenever you can.

> I will go to great lengths to avoid advertising. I love to go to the movies, and my son shares my love of film. Whenever we go to the cinema, I wait in the foyer reading a book while he goes in to watch the trailers and adverts. He then texts me when the film is about to start, and only then do I go in!

SOCIAL MEDIA

We have already established that we tend to compare ourselves to those better off than us. When it comes to social media, that comparison is often based on false pretences and can be a major source of comparison unhappiness.

We tend to only put the best side of ourselves out to the public. Photographs of the wonderful meal, the fabulous night out with friends, hashtags such as #winning or #boom. Influencers, who can make huge money by building up followers of the happy and glamorous lifestyle they portray on social media, often end up burnt out or suffering mental health issues from having to constantly keep up the pretence.[117]

Social media is not reality. There is always someone who seems to be richer or better or faster or prettier or more successful. Social media has heightened our tendency to compare up. If we can develop a habit of comparing down, or not at all, if we can condition ourselves not to judge our situation by reference to the situation of others, then we can start to find joy in where we are.

In a presentation, my friend and behavioural expert Neil Bage uses a picture of a beautiful happy baby to illustrate this point – the sort of picture you often see on Facebook. On the next slide, we zoom out a little to see the baby surrounded by clutter.

And on the third slide we zoom out further to see the total picture, including an extremely harassed mum. Only the first picture gets shared on social media. Neil discusses this on *The Financial Wellbeing Podcast*.[118]

Curating your social media experience may be a solution to the negativity we feel from social comparison. When I hear someone berating Twitter for being so negative, for example, I remind them that the messages they are receiving are coming from people that they have chosen to follow. What you read on social media is what you choose to read.

Spending time deciding what you want to see may reduce the degree to which you compare up to unrealistic images of others. This will enable your financial wellbeing plan to be about what brings *you* joy.

LIFESTYLE CREEP

'Lifestyle creep' is a term that describes how, as we *earn* more money, we *spend* more money, with the result that we never seem to have any left at the end of the month.

This is connected with the 'hedonic adaptation' concept, which we looked at in *Chapter 10*. We have a tendency to return to our stable level of wellbeing despite what life throws at us. But, and this is where this theory applies to lifestyle creep, this also means that, as we make more money so our expectations and desires rise.

If we get a pay rise, or a bonus, it is tempting to think of this as 'free' money and to spend it. Instead, anchor your thoughts back to your intrinsic motivations; think of your future self. Can you put money into one of your allocated savings or investment pots? Is there a debt to repay that will get you to your intrinsic motivations quicker?

> Maria Nedeva found that her husband had built up a huge debt on credit cards without her knowing – over £100,000. She vowed to pay it off as quickly as she could, taking extra jobs and saving furiously. All the spare money she could find went towards paying down this debt.
>
> The smallest amount of the debt that she paid off was £2.60. It was this total dedication to the plan that enabled her to repay the entire debt within a staggering two years.[119]

IT'S GOOD TO TALK

Simonne Gnessen has been a financial coach, and trainer of financial coaches, for 20 years. I think of her as the godmother of financial coaching in the UK. In researching this book, I asked Simonne what she views as the biggest blockage to achieving financial well-being plans. I quote her response in full:

> My major bugbear is the secrecy around money. People spending money they can't afford, in order to keep up appearances, living beyond their means, and burying their heads in the sand until it's too late... The myth is that it's not polite (or that it is inappropriate) to talk about money, in many cases even between couples. I'm forever trying to spread the message that if we can talk openly with friends and family about subjects like food or health or relationships, then why not money? Yes, we have to overcome the emotion surrounding the subject, but I believe we can live more authentic, fulfilling lives if we are able to face up to our feelings about money.[120]

THE ULTIMATE
SELF-LIMITING BELIEF

There is one final belief that we must address. One that brings us full circle in creating our financial wellbeing plan. It is a belief that is at the heart of so much misery and unhappiness in the world, yet it is almost universally accepted as being a truth.

It is the belief that more money will make you more happy.

This is surely the ultimate self-limiting belief.

This belief is self-limiting for a number of reasons. Getting more money (or accumulating more 'stuff') is, for many people, unattainable. Striving for something that is unattainable can only lead to unhappiness. It is about 'more' versus 'enough.'

Being able to acquire more money is often out of our control. Whether we chase pay rises or play the lottery, whether we come into money is not always a result of our own actions.

This belief is never ending. It is like seeing the top of the mountain only to find that there is a further peak beyond, and another beyond that. Always more.

Finally, this belief is not a truth. We have looked at many research models that show this, including set point theory, Maslow's hierarchy of needs, the teachings of Buddhism, the longitudinal Harvard study on happiness, and so on. From university research to psychology to philosophers to spiritual guidance, the evidence is everywhere. More money does not *automatically* make you more happy, and there comes a point beyond which no amount of money will make you more happy.

This is a question that this book seeks to answer: where is that line? How much is enough for *you*? By making your intrinsic motivations your starting point, you can turn your financial plan into a financial wellbeing plan.

If you strip away the money distractions and start to 'know thyself,' to understand what brings *you* wellbeing, the focus away from 'more' may well reveal that 'enough' is a lot closer than you thought.

CHAPTER 13

●●●●

BRINGING IT ALL TOGETHER

We have seen how a plan for wellbeing should start with understanding that joy comes from self-worth – from intrinsic motivations. We have seen that self-worth comes from compassion, helping others. These are the things that bring meaning and purpose into our lives.

> Robert Waldinger is director of the Harvard Study of Adult Development, the long-term study on happiness first mentioned in *Chapter 4*. In an interview he commented on one aspect of the findings of the study: "There is a lot to be said for achievement if what you're doing is meaningful to you. What we find is that the badges of achievement don't make people happy. We had people who were CEOs, who made lots of money, or who became famous. Those things did not relate to happiness."[121]

I suggested in *Chapter 1* that recognising these sources of joy represents Steps Two and Three in our three-step plan. We have looked at the evidence behind these steps, as well as considering the barriers to achieving them.

Now that you have a better understanding of the wellbeing that lies in waiting, you can finally embark on *Step One*: work through the appendices to create your own financial wellbeing plan.

APPENDIX 1:
YOUR FINANCIAL WELLBEING PLAN

As you read through the book, you will be directed to this appendix often. You might choose to read through the book first to gain an understanding of the principles of financial wellbeing, then read through it a second time, completing these exercises as you go.

These activities are designed to help you prepare your financial wellbeing plan. This is different from a financial plan, which focuses on the money. The financial wellbeing plan focuses on your life – your wellbeing – and as such works alongside or as part of your financial plan (which you or your financial adviser will create separately). This gives your financial plan direction, so that the outcome of the two plans together is to help you to use your money to accumulate life, not the other way around.

If you already have your own financial plan, then you might use the output from the activities that follow to review where that plan is taking you. If you do not have a financial plan, then the output from these activities will help you to set your objectives. Either way, these exercises will also guide you in reviewing your relationship with money.

If you are able to engage a financial planner to assist you, then take the output of this plan to them. Alternatively, if your financial planner has taken training in coaching skills (e.g. if they have completed the Financial Wellbeing Certificate offered by the Institute for Financial Wellbeing[122]), then they will be able to help you to complete this plan.

Another tip is to keep returning to this plan on a regular (perhaps annual) basis. When you do review the plan, don't overwrite what you decided previously – add to the plan. In this way you will build a record of the actions you have taken to improve your financial wellbeing, which will enable you to reflect on what has worked and what has not.

PLAN OVERVIEW

Let's remind ourselves of the five pillars of financial wellbeing:
- A clear path to identifiable objectives
- Being able to cope with financial shocks
- Having financial options
- Control of daily finances
- Clarity and security for those that we leave behind

The exercises that follow are arranged in the same order in which they arrive throughout the text. I have added a note for each to show to which of the five pillars it relates (I have separated the first pillar into 'A clear path' and 'Identifying objectives').

Together, these activities will help you to compile your financial wellbeing plan. There is no template to follow; these activities are designed to help you reflect on what brings meaning and purpose to your life and how your relationship to money can foster this. You may choose to keep the outputs in one document or to apply them in different places.

EXERCISE 1:
YOUR DEFINITION
OF SUCCESS

From "Your Definition of Success" in *Chapter 2*
Identifying objectives

To help you find a definition of success that might be right for you, go through this three-part exercise.[123]

PART 1: WHOM DO YOU ADMIRE?

Write down three people whom you admire. You might want to include someone you know and maybe someone who might be considered famous.

Now write down what it is you like and admire about them. Take your time – list as many things as you can.

Are there any common themes? Any particular attributes that you realise crop up more than once? Could you make a list of, say, four of the most common attributes?

Now set aside the names of the people you have chosen and just keep the list of attributes.

Now consider this list. These attributes are likely to also describe you, or who you aspire to be.

This part of the exercise is intended to generate some ideas for you to ponder. Some attributes may be a mirror of you, reflecting back to you values you have that you most treasure. Some of them may bring out feelings of guilt because you are *not* like that. Others may be what you would aspire to be like, but something is currently preventing you.

Just take some time to reflect on the list without drawing too many conclusions.

PART 2: LEARNING FROM YOUR PAST

Write down some of the moments in your life that you consider to have been the most joyful. They might be big or they might be fleeting.

Now write down some of the moments in your life that carry the most regret. Again, they could be big or small.

Consider this list, and ask yourself the following question: what were the drivers or emotions behind these moments? Reflecting on these moments, see if you can write down some values that run deep within you and that might suggest why you chose those moments.

PART 3: LOOKING FOR CORRELATION

Put the outcomes from parts 1 and 2 in front of you.

Now ask yourself these questions:
- Does your relationship to your money have any impact on these drivers or emotions?
- Are you using your money to help create more of the joyful moments?
- Are you using your money to help create *less* of the regrettable moments?

Write down any conclusions that you draw from this exercise so far.

YOUR DEFINITION

Now write down your definition of success. It might be a sentence or it could be a list. It's yours, so you choose! Don't worry if it is still a guess or you don't feel you've captured it exactly – we're not looking for a perfect slogan, just to get some ideas down to provide some structure to your financial wellbeing plan.

You'll probably be changing your definition over time. If you do, don't delete the old one, just cross it out. It might be interesting to look back on how your thinking might have changed!

EXERCISE 2:
CREATING A DECISION MATRIX

From "Short-Term Pain for Long-Term Gain" in *Chapter 3*
Daily finances

To recap, our instinct is to avoid delaying gratification; we prefer our happiness now. This tendency to prioritise the present over the future is sometimes at the expense of our future selves.

In order to overcome this instinct, consider putting in place rules that will prevent you from reacting to situations and keep your money habits aligned with your financial plan. Examples of financial rules that you might want to consider include:

- Set up regular payments. For example, if you don't have an emergency fund, set up a small, affordable regular payment into a savings account – a level that you know you will not be tempted to cancel. Do the same for other future expenses, such as holidays.
- Set up a regular date to look at your financial plan (either on your own or at a meeting with your financial planner).
- Don't sign up to automatic renewals. If it is an option, ensure any policy that renews each year (such as car insurance) requires your authorisation, to prompt you to search the market for a better price.

- If you're part of a workplace pension scheme, check to see its matching options. Could you increase your automatic monthly pension contributions and also get an additional amount added by your employer?

You will probably be able to think of many more. The simple principle is to find something that you know you should do but that you tend not to, only to regret it later. Can that decision be automated?

Remember – as well as taking action, write down what you have done on your plan. It may provide you with some comfort in a few years' time to look back and see how far you have come.

EXERCISE 3: CONNECTING WITH YOUR FUTURE SELF

From "Connecting with Your Future Self" in *Chapter 3*[124]
A clear path

To recap, when we think of our future self, we use the part of the brain that we use when we think of other people. In order to encourage ourselves to take action now, we need to better connect with our future selves.

Our objective with this exercise is therefore to connect with our future self on a meaningful level – to make our future self feel like it is, indeed, us.

We will focus this connection on three levels:
- Physical
- Emotional
- Pathway

Remember, though – this future self is not to be cast in concrete. Plans *will* change, and this needs to be accepted. You are trying to make a connection, but not one that is so rigid that you will be unable to deviate from it. You may wish to go through this exercise on a regular (annual?) basis.

PHYSICAL

You might consider an ageing app to produce a picture of yourself at a future point, such as your preferred retirement age. When you look at this picture, ask yourself this general question: when I am looking like this, how do I want to be living? Seeing an aged version of yourself is not comfortable for everyone, however, so only use this if it works for you.

Another idea is to picture your future. Maybe close your eyes, and imagine yourself waking up and looking around your room. What does your home look like? Are you living with someone? You open the windows, what do you see? What are you going to do that day? What about in the evening, or at the weekend? What does your social life include? Be optimistic, but also realistic.

You might choose to write some of this down. The idea is to feel that there is a future you can imagine and feel connected with.

EMOTIONAL

Once you have considered the future in practical terms, set aside some time to consider your future in terms of your emotional reaction. This could be by asking the question "At this point in the future, what does a good day look like?" Perhaps repeat the 'Physical' part of the exercise, but now consider issues such as where you will be getting meaning and purpose from.

If you will no longer be receiving purpose and community from home (e.g. because your kids will have left) or work (e.g. if you will have retired), where *will* this be coming from?

Another idea is to consider role models.[125] Can you think of who you would consider as a role model, that you would like to be more like? Think about what they do, what they say, how they behave. Imagine yourself acting and behaving in that way.

PATHWAY

It is also important to feel a realistic connection to your future self – that there is a series of steps to follow that might take you there.

You might be able to put a financial price on some of these things that you envisage, in order to gain clarity over how much you need to save for your future self. In this way, you will create that clear path. This could then be taken to your financial planner, if you have one.

The more clearly that you can imagine yourself in the future, the greater connection you will have to your future self. In this way, the more motivated you will be to take action on your financial plan now. Remember, though, these plans are likely to change, so clarity over your future self is important, alongside flexibility to deviate to a better plan if you were to find one.

EXERCISE 4:
ASSESSING YOUR BALANCE
OF WELLBEING

From "The Five Elements of Wellbeing We Can Influence" in
Chapter 8
Financial options

This exercise is intended to prompt you to give some thought to your balance of wellbeing. Is one of the five elements of wellbeing dominating the others? By recognising where there may be an imbalance, you may find that you have more financial options than you previously believed.

STEP 1

List the five elements of wellbeing on a piece of paper. Give each of them a score of importance, in an ideal world. One way of doing this might be to create a pie chart as below. Simply draw a line across each segment at a level that represents how important each is to you, with a line near the outer edge signifying more importance than a line near the middle.

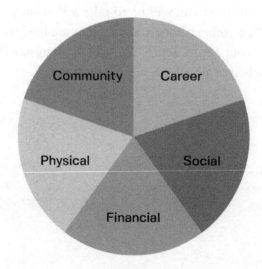

STEP 2

Look at these five elements again. Now (maybe with a different colour of pen) give them a score on their *current* level in your life. Compare this with Step 1. Are there any conclusions you might draw?

STEP 3

If appropriate, get your partner to go through Steps 1 and 2, without sharing your results. Now compare your outcomes with theirs. Are there any new conclusions that you might draw?

STEP 4

Remember that the quality of social relationships is the largest contributor to overall wellbeing. How do your scores compare here? If you are going to take any remedial action, then any discrepancies in this area may be a good place to start.

STEP 5

Of those five elements of wellbeing, the only one that doesn't directly add to wellbeing is financial wellbeing. Reflect again on the results of this exercise, and ask yourself one key question: is your financial plan helping the other four elements, or does it focus on accumulating wealth and status?

EXERCISE 5:
COPING WITH
FINANCIAL SHOCKS

From "Money and Happiness" in *Chapter 8*
Financial shocks

In one survey, 69% of the respondents didn't have any of the following: life assurance, critical illness cover or income protection.[126]

Given that a) knowing you will be able to cope with a financial shock and b) knowing that you have security for those you leave behind are two of the five pillars of financial wellbeing, getting suitable protection should be a relatively simple way to reduce stress. At the time of writing, life assurance for 20 years, for a male and female couple aged 30, to pay out £200,000 on the first to die, would cost just less than £12 per month.[127]

Knowing that you have a little cash put away as an emergency fund will provide wellbeing. In an ideal world, you should have an instantly accessible cash fund of between three and six months' normal expenditure. If this is not possible right now, then start paying whatever is possible into such a fund. Even a small amount each month will build up in time, and give you some peace of mind.

EXERCISE 6:
CLARITY AND SECURITY FOR THOSE THAT WE LEAVE BEHIND

From "Money and Happiness" in *Chapter 8*

Clarity and security

If you have children, write a will. That's it! If you have assets to leave behind, then using a will writer or solicitor is always going to be best. But even a simple will downloaded from the internet is better than leaving it to the courts to decide what happens to your children in the event of your death.

If you do have an estate to leave, regardless of size, then you may wish to give some thought as to how this might be used by your successors. If this is of concern to you, then you might consider developing a family constitution – a set of values and beliefs shared by all of your family. This can be incredibly useful in instructing future generations in the case of disagreements, and it can be especially appropriate for family businesses. Family constitutions are a very specialist area. If this is of interest, you should consider taking specialist advice.

Be open to having a conversation with your family about your wishes, and informing them of where your financial details are held. If you have one, introduce your financial planner to any adult children so they know who to talk to when you are gone.

EXERCISE 7:
EXERCISE FOR BUSINESS OWNERS

From "The Danger of Goals" in *Chapter 9*
Financial options

Many business owners are so focused on their business that they do not take the time to look up and see where they are going. Their self-worth and sense of purpose become intrinsically related to the business. As a result, the business often suffers as they struggle to give up control and find it difficult to leave. Their options become limited as they are bound up with the business.

Take a moment to reflect on these questions:
- How well do your current and future plans for your business help you to achieve your personal aims?
- To what extent do you find meaning and purpose in what you do in your business?
- How would you replace this if the business were sold?
- To what extent does the impact of your business (e.g. customer and employee outcomes) align with your intrinsic motivations?
- How does your business help you achieve the five elements of financial wellbeing?

The ultimate question every business owner should be able to answer is:
- How much do you *need* your business to be worth?

Not what is the value – but how much do you need? Your financial planner, with the help of cashflow forecasting, should be able to help you answer this question. Only when you have this information can you truly make plans for your business, and therefore your life.

EXERCISE 8:
IDENTIFYING PURPOSE

From "Identifying What Makes You Happy" in *Chapter 9*
Identifying objectives

We know that wellbeing comes from intrinsic motivations, which we might also describe as living a life with meaning and purpose. We also know that helping others and showing compassion are sources of wellbeing.

With this in mind, ask yourself: what brings you purpose? What would you *like* to do that would bring you purpose?

Imagine you win the lottery. Enough so that you know you won't need to work again. Now think of yourself a year later. You've bought the house and the big car; you've been to Machu Picchu, or to watch Barcelona at Camp Nou. You are now sitting on the sofa looking at the bucket list you drew up just after the big win. Each item on the bucket list has a big tick by it. The new day stretches out in front of you. What are you going to do with it?

What would make you jump out of bed if you didn't need to earn? This might not be a simple question to answer, so take your time (to repeat, your financial planner may be able to help with this question if they have coaching training). Maybe it's your current job or the business you run; maybe it's something charitable, making a difference to other people.

Just write down some options. Be as specific as possible, but don't stop when you only have one idea. This is all about creating options.

EXERCISE 9:
IDENTIFYING PURPOSE –
SELF-DETERMINATION THEORY TEST

From "Identifying What Makes You Happy" in *Chapter 9*
Identifying objectives

Reflect on the results of some of these exercises, such as the list of options you created from Exercise 8. What would need to happen for you to start making some of those options become real?

Apply the three components of self-determination theory:
- Do you (or can you) have competence in the thing?
- Will you have autonomy to do the thing?
- Can you see how the thing relates to others?

Apply them to how you spend your time – perhaps your job, or any community work you are involved with. Does this reveal anything to you about what changes you might want to make? Or about how great things currently are?! It's important when creating your plans to build on what is working for you, not just seek to change what is not.

Apply the three components to your intrinsic motivations – things that you want to do that will bring you meaning and purpose. What needs to happen for these three elements to be in place?

Now apply the three components to your retirement plans, if this is your priority. What will you do in retirement that will bring you these three elements?

EXERCISE 10:
IDENTIFYING CORE VALUES

From "Identifying Your Core Values" in *Chapter 9*
Identifying objectives

This exercise is intended to help you identify your core values so you can better connect with your future self.

Firstly, write down what you think your core values are. Choose no more than five from the following list (keeping the number low means you will be forced to prioritise).

Achievement, Adventure, Authenticity, Authority, Autonomy, Balance, Boldness, Compassion, Challenge, Citizenship, Community, Competency, Creativity, Curiosity, Determination, Fairness, Faith, Fame, Friendships, Fun, Growth, Happiness, Honesty, Humour, Influence, Inner Harmony, Justice, Kindness, Knowledge, Leadership, Learning, Love, Loyalty, Meaningful Work, Openness, Optimism, Peace, Pleasure, Poise, Popularity, Professionalism, Recognition, Religion, Reputation, Respect, Responsibility, Self-Respect, Service, Spirituality, Stability, Status, Success, Trustworthiness, Wisdom.

Now answer the following question. Imagine you are able to listen in on your own funeral. One of your oldest friends is waiting to go into the service. The previous service has finished, and your friend spots someone they know. They go over and say hi to each other.

After a few brief pleasantries, the other person asks your friend whose funeral they are attending. The other person doesn't know you, and so they ask a follow-up question: "Who were they?"

How *will* your friend answer?

How would you *like* them to have answered?

EXERCISE 11:
THE FINANCIAL WELLBEING JUNKIE

From "The Financial Wellbeing Junkie" in *Chapter 10*
Daily finances

We all buy things that we don't need in order to give ourselves a quick pick-me-up. When reviewing our spending, we should consider whether this habit is creating a problem, for example stopping us from achieving our financial plan.

Try this exercise. It involves working out how much money you have available to spend – then working it out again![128] Follow this process:

1. Review your spending, separating it into categories (of your choosing, but you might use 'essential food,' 'non-essential food,' 'essential clothing,' 'non-essential clothing' and so on). The point is to get an idea of:
   › How much you need to spend to live (rent or mortgage payments)
   › How much you need to spend for your wellbeing (e.g. a holiday or spending time with friends and family)
   › How much is for your future self
   › How much is genuinely unnecessary spending that doesn't add to your wellbeing
2. How much do you spend in each month in that last category?
3. Consider the results of all of the previous exercises, especially the ones relating to intrinsic motivations and connecting to your future self
4. Reflect on how much of your budget you allocate to bringing that future closer
5. Go back to the start and review your spending – can any of the luxuries and 'nice-to-have' spending be reallocated to the future without causing a major reduction in your wellbeing now?

EXERCISE 12:
PHILANTHROPY PLAN

From "Wellbeing from Giving" in *Chapter 10*

A clear path

The work you have already undertaken about meaning and purpose, and assessing your values, should have given you some insight into the things that really matter to you. You can use this to assess charities, clubs, projects or anything else to which you may wish to consider giving your time and/or money.

Develop your own personal philanthropy plan. By making a plan, and sticking to it, your giving can come from a position of joy, rather than guilt. Below are a few ideas for how to create your own plan for giving.

OPTION 1: MAKING A REGULAR GIFT

If you are looking to make a regular financial gift, decide how much you might be able to give on a monthly basis.

Next, search for a list of charities.[129] Make a list of some of the charities that you think might interest you. Now, with your core values in front of you, look at their websites and in particular the 'mission' or 'about us' section. Create a shortlist of those that align with your values. You might now decide to which of these charities you could set up a regular donation.

OPTION 2: MAKING A SINGLE LARGE DONATION

If you can make a larger, one-off donation, decide how much this might be (a cashflow forecast can help with this).

Search for a list of local charities.[130] Repeat Option 1's exercise of comparing your core values with their mission.

You might now make a one-off donation, or perhaps include a bequest in your will. If it is a large donation, get in touch with the charity or community foundation to discuss it with them.

OPTION 3: YOUR PERSONAL COMMUNITY PLAN

Write down a list of things that interest you locally. This might include sports clubs, wildlife trusts, music groups, healthcare services, charity shops, schools and many, many other entities! What opportunities do they have for you to get involved?

Again, compare these opportunities with your values. Additionally, do any of the charities on your list align with your skill set and/or preferred activities? For example, your child might play a sport at a local club, or perhaps you already play at a sports club that has a junior section, and you could get involved organising or coaching.

Next, work out how much time you have to give. Be realistic – you don't want to over-commit, but you also might not want to rule out an evening or two just because your favourite TV show is on!

Next, get in touch with the organisations that seem to have the best fit for your abilities, your interests and your time. Find out how you might be able to help.

Finalise your shortlist by assessing each option using the self-determination criteria introduced in *Exercise 9*:
- Do you (or can you) have competence in the thing?
- Will you have autonomy to do the thing?
- Can you see how the thing relates to others?

Perhaps score each opportunity out of ten on the above criteria, plus whether they are a good fit with your core values. You should now have a league table of opportunities to give your time to.

As with all plans, you should set a date for it to be reviewed. If you have a financial planner, then you could share this plan with them and make the review of your philanthropy plan part of your annual meeting.

EXERCISE 13:
WELLBEING FROM DELAYED
GRATIFICATION

From "Delayed Consumption" in *Chapter 10*
Daily finances

STEP 1
Write down your short-term financial goals. Although your plan aims to use money to increase intrinsic motivations, we still need to enjoy ourselves in the short term. We know that greater wellbeing is derived from experiences with loved ones and friends, such as tickets to events and holidays, than from buying 'stuff.'

Add pictures representing those short-term goals. You might also do this for your longer-term intrinsic motivations, if they are clear to you.

STEP 2
If you are tempted to buy something that isn't actually necessary, something you might think of as a bit of a treat, just wait a week. In that week, look at the pictures from Step 1. If you still want to buy that item after that week, then go ahead. You probably really want it!

If it is a major item, you might set up a saving plan rather than taking finance. For example, if a shop offers an item costing £300 to be paid in "ten easy payments of £30," could you wait ten months and put £30 away each month instead?

As well as being a way of combating that financial wellbeing junkie urge, this is a form of delaying consumption. You are deciding not to consume the item straight away but to wait, and, if it's something you really want, you will have the joy of anticipation. In that period, however, you may well compare buying the thing with the holiday brochure that you've got stuck to your computer at work, and decide to put the money towards the holiday or another intrinsic motivation instead.

EXERCISE 14: BEHAVIOURAL BIASES – ENDOWMENT EFFECT

From "Endowment Effect" in *Chapter 11*
Identifying objectives

If you find these various 'know thyself' exercises rather difficult, it might be because you feel reluctant to let go of what you currently have – which may be down to the endowment effect.

Take a look at the outcomes of the exercises above. Now ask the following questions (or get someone to ask them of you):
- What do you see as success?
- What will happen once you have achieved that success?
- What makes you proud?
- What is it about 'that' that makes you proud?
- When are you happiest?
- What do you get a buzz from?
- Is there anything else you would like to get a buzz from in retirement?

Then, when you have some of these answers, ask:
- How do you see yourself doing those things?

EXERCISE 15:
SELF-LIMITING BELIEFS

From "Self-Limiting Beliefs" in Chapter 12[131]
Financial options

PART 1
For a period of, say, two weeks, write down any thoughts you have relating to money. Don't dwell upon them – just write them down when they pop into your head. Maybe it is when you buy something as a treat, or don't buy something because you think it is a waste of money. Perhaps it's a reaction to something you see on the news, or a discussion with a family member or friend. Just compile a list of things that come into your mind in relation to money.

PART 2
Once you have a list of your money thoughts, dedicate some time to reviewing them. Find a quiet spot, turn off the TV or radio, put your phone on silent and don't look at social media.

Spend some time with each of the thoughts you have written down. Can you spot consistency between the thoughts? Are there any money 'beliefs' that start to emerge? Write these down in a separate list.

Ask yourself the following questions about each of these beliefs:
- What experience brought about this belief?
- What evidence do I have to confirm that this belief is true?

- How does this belief affect my financial decisions?
- Is this belief benefitting me?

If the answers suggest that a belief may be self-limiting, then you might continue and ask the following questions:
- Is there a different belief that might replace this one?
- Will that new belief help me make better financial decisions?
- What do I have to do to make sure this new belief replaces the old belief?

EXERCISE 16:
PERMISSION

From "Permission" in *Chapter 12*[132]
Financial options

This exercise is intended to help you to assess whether a lack of permission is preventing you from making better financial decisions – and to provide a structure for how you might change this if so.

Take some time to step back and reflect on how you are allocating your money and your time. Look at your calendar and at your bank accounts. Write out how you have been spending your time and how you spend your money. Maybe some themes will present themselves, allowing you to group your actions. After a while, your list will show you what have been your priorities.

Now review that list in light of this question: are your choices about how you are spending your time and money for you, or for other people? To put this another away, are your activities aligned to your values, to your intrinsic motivations?

If you have examples of your activities not being aligned with your values, ask what is driving that choice. Ask yourself what you would be willing to do differently. Are these your decisions?

CONCLUDING YOUR FINANCIAL WELLBEING PLAN

At the end of these exercises, you may well have a bunch of notes, thoughts and ideas. Hopefully you have a bit more clarity over what wellbeing means *for you.*

The objective is to create a financial wellbeing plan that makes you happier and healthier, not just wealthier. This will be achieved by reducing the stress you feel when making financial decisions. This may also increase your motivation to undertake financial planning.

Your financial wellbeing plan should aim to achieve each of the following to some extent:
- Positive action to overcome your natural instincts (where they are working against your wellbeing)
- Better understanding of the relationship between money and happiness, and what brings joy to your life (notably helping others, and the quality of your social relationships)
- Understanding of where your own individual behavioural biases and self-limiting beliefs may be sabotaging your plans
- A better connection with your future self
- Understanding of your intrinsic motivations (meaning and purpose)

You could sense-check your plan by answering the following questions:

- What are my achievable intrinsic motivations?
- Does my plan increase some or all of the five pillars of financial wellbeing?
- Does my plan result in a balance of the five elements of wellbeing that is right for me?
- Who else does my plan affect?

In this way, your financial wellbeing plan should help you to develop a better relationship with money, where money is an engine for wellbeing, not a barrier to it.

APPENDIX 2:
HOW TO GENERATE THE HAPPY CHEMICALS

There are four chemicals in the brain that contribute to our feeling happy. We all seek short-term hits of happiness in order to keep us to our set-point level of wellbeing (as outlined in *Chapter 10*).

As a result of reading about these chemicals, you may wish to reflect on your lifestyle, and in particular how you are allocating your money and your time. Consider whether you might do more to produce these chemicals and whether this could enable you to reduce your spending on 'financial wellbeing junkie'-type items.[133]

ENDORPHINS

Endorphins relieve pain or stress. Here are things you might do to release endorphins:
- *Exercise*. This could be playing a sport or going to the gym, but it could also be a brisk walk Note: exercise has a positive impact on *all four* happiness chemicals.

- *Acupuncture.* Research has shown that acupuncture triggers the brain to release endorphins.
- *Meditation.* A focus on your thoughts and breathing well.
- *Playing music.* This includes singing, dancing or playing an instrument – even more so when with others, which also benefits the community aspect of wellbeing.
- *Laughter.* Laughter also increases levels of serotonin and dopamine.
- *Sunshine on the skin.* Ultraviolet light releases beta-endorphins in the skin.
- *Physical contact.* One study revealed that having sex once or twice a week boosts our immune system (but three or more times had the opposite effect!).[134]

DOPAMINE

As dopamine is part of the brain's reward system, having a daily to-do list and crossing things off when you get them done is good for dopamine. Being creative is good for dopamine, and also for endorphins.

Being involved with something that has great purpose, giving a sense of achievement as well as community wellbeing, will have a positive effect. This might mean giving time, perhaps by getting involved in something locally, whether that be a sports club, a charity or something else where you can get a sense of achievement.

Diet also has a part to play, as dopamine is made from tyrosine, an amino acid that is especially high in chicken, dairy, avocadoes, bananas, pumpkin and sesame seeds, and soy.

SEROTONIN

Anti-depressants aim to increase the amount of serotonin in the brain. However, there are several ways to increase serotonin without drugs, including:

- Sunlight
- Aerobic exercise
- Diet, notably foods high in tryptophan, such as chicken, eggs, cheese, peanuts, pumpkin and sesame seeds... and chocolate![135]

OXYTOCIN

Sometimes called the 'love hormone,' oxytocin is boosted by physical contact. This could be as simple as giving or receiving a massage, or having a hug.

Playing music collaboratively or singing in a group leads to bonding and sharing, which boosts oxytocin. We could extend this to being linked with a community. Having a pet – and giving it lots of love and cuddles – has been shown to lower blood pressure and increase oxytocin.[136]

APPENDIX 3:
HOW DO I FIND A FINANCIAL ADVISER WHO IS RIGHT FOR ME?

There are many ways to obtain face-to-face financial advice in the UK, and a rather bewildering array of descriptors have evolved over the past few years. Here is a summary of the various sources of advice, including what to expect from each of them. Some firms may have more than one of these types of adviser (e.g. a larger firm may have both wealth managers and financial planners).

As a key part of financial wellbeing is creating "a clear path to achievable intrinsic motivations" (as argued in *Chapter 8*), I would always suggest you choose a financial adviser who is proficient in using cashflow forecasting. There are a number of cashflow forecasting software providers that advisers use, each with their own strengths and weaknesses. An adviser who doesn't provide cashflow forecasting is not going to be as proficient in helping you create your clear path, if that is what you need.

One type of adviser is not necessarily better than any other type of adviser. They simply offer different things. It is therefore important that you get the type of adviser who is right for *you*.

INDEPENDENT FINANCIAL ADVISER (IFA)

An overarching term that describes most UK financial advisers. They are regulated by the Financial Conduct Authority (FCA), and you can expect them to adhere to standards of ethics. You will also have access to compensation schemes in the unlikely event they are needed. The 'independent' means that they are free to recommend financial products from the whole of the market, not being restricted to those offered by a limited number of providers.

RESTRICTED ADVISER

A restricted adviser can only recommend from a limited range of financial products, often just ones that are offered by their own company. They are also regulated by the FCA. The adviser should make it plain that they are restricted; however, this is not always the case, and therefore you may wish to ask in order to be certain.

FINANCIAL PLANNER

An adviser who describes themselves as a financial planner should use cashflow forecasting and be focused on helping you work out your future, in addition to offering advice on financial products. You may also want to ask if they have had any coaching skills training. Financial planners will usually be regulated by the FCA. They are a few who are not, and those ones will not be able to offer advice on investment products, pensions and so on.

WEALTH MANAGER

This is likely to describe somebody who is focused on managing investments. They may also give tax advice.

FINANCIAL COACH/MONEY COACH

A non-regulated coach will be an expert in helping you with your relationship with money. They may or may not also provide financial planning. Ensure that they have had formal training and hold a qualification in financial coaching. Use a financial coach where you don't need investment, tax or pension advice, but do need help with how you deal with money.

FINANCIAL ADVISER SPECIALISING IN WELLBEING

If you have already read this book, you will now know that 'financial wellbeing' is a term that describes a very broad topic, encompassing all aspects of our relationship to money. Some firms, however, have adopted the term simply for marketing purposes, and do not deliver financial wellbeing in practice. Others use it to describe how you manage your money (which I would call 'financial resilience'). If you want an expert in this book's broad definition of financial wellbeing, you should expect them to be a member of the Institute for Financial Wellbeing (IFW) and preferably to have passed the Financial Wellbeing Certificate, which the IFW offers.

APPENDIX 4:
A NOTE FOR FINANCIAL ADVISERS (OTHER READERS ALSO WELCOME!)

Although this book is aimed at the general public, it can also act as a manual for financial advisers and planners. You might like to read this section before embarking on the book.

> You'll see a number of 'Tips for financial advisers' along the way, in these boxes.

I hope you might read the book with this thought constantly in mind: "How can I bring this into my financial planning process?"

This might not, however, be as easy to do as you might at first think.

When a person engages a financial adviser, I would suggest that they invariably have one objective in particular: to hand the responsibility of their money over to somebody else.

As this book explores, money is a fearful thing, because it relates to the unknown. Creating a financial plan requires a person to enter the unknown in two ways: because of their lack of expertise about money, and in terms of how a financial decision now might play out in the future.

When a client hands over their finances for you to look after, what they are saying is: "Please could you take care of this for me? It scares me. I don't know enough about it to be able to make sensible decisions, nor do I know enough about my future to know what the best thing is. So please, could you look after my money, so I can get on with living my best life?"

In response, what do finance advisers do?

They typically bring the client back into the meeting room in order to tell them all about the money. The share the knowledge they have worked hard to attain about investment principles, pension rules, tax rules and so on.

In other words, financial advisers tend to talk to clients about the one thing the clients do not want to hear about.

Why might this be?

THE MOST IMPORTANT
PERSON IN THE ROOM

When you go and see a specialist doctor, a consultant or perhaps a surgeon, who is the most important person in the room?

Picture the scene. You sit with your partner, nervously awaiting the results of your tests. The consultant comes in, perhaps asks how you're feeling for a bit of small talk, and then provides you with the benefit of their considerable knowledge and experience. They tell you what they have discovered, and provide you with their advice.

The meeting is centred around their expertise. *They* are the most important person in the room – or so everyone present believes.

This is how many financial advisers conduct their client meetings. Indeed, it is how we are educated to act.

PROBLEM SOLVING

All through our lives we are taught to solve problems. Through school and through professional exams we are given questions or problems and tasked to find a solution.

Knowledge in such an environment tends to be somewhat black and white. There are people who know the answer and people who do not know the answer – experts and non-experts. Education under such parameters is then the process of imparting that knowledge from the former to the latter.

Knowledge needs context, and this is especially true of money. We each have our own histories. One person may have an illness because of poor diet, whereas in another the same illness may be caused by stress. That consultant might prescribe the same medicine to treat the illness, despite the cause being completely different.

Due to the fact that we are trained to solve problems, we tend to see clients as problems that need solving. We are tempted to rush towards a solution as fast as our little legs can carry us.

Often, however, what a client really needs is help in defining the problem. And this is *very* often the case with financial planning.

A client who comes for a pension review will often get a pension review. What actually prompted them to see a financial adviser, however, may well have been that they were doing a job that did not fulfil them, they were bullied by their boss, and they wanted to do a job that gave them pride and meaning that paid less money, but they didn't know if they could afford it.

Would your meeting with the client have brought this information out?

WHAT 'CLIENT FOCUSED' REALLY MEANS

There is one tool in the financial adviser's toolkit that, in my experience, is often used the least: silence. The answer you get immediately is usually the System 1 answer (see *Chapter 3*), the one the client thinks you want to hear. Leave that space, by just keeping quiet, and the next thing the client says is more likely to be a System 2 answer: one that is deeper and more thoughtful.

The most important person in the meeting room is the client. Your years of experience and technical knowledge count for nothing in comparison with the life of the client in front of you. "You are a student of your client."[137]

That's not to say that your knowledge and experience are not important – technical knowledge is crucial to delivering great client outcomes. It's just that, I'd suggest, it should be kept to a minimum in the meeting room.

Being client focused means listening. It means uncovering objectives that are not goals but that are intrinsic motivations. These are skills that need to be acquired, that require training.

> I was talking to the head of compliance of a large UK network that provides compliance and support services to hundreds of financial advisory firms and thousands of advisers. I commented that the 'Objectives' sections of most client reports were not objectives at all. I joked that some 90% of those sections were a variant on "Your objectives are to access our investment proposition in order to obtain above-market investment returns." Furthermore, I offered, this is not even an objective, it is an outcome.
>
> The head of compliance said that he disagreed with me. He was the one who oversaw the reviews of those client reports. In his opinion, the figure was not 90%.
>
> He said the figure was far closer to 100%!

Being client focused means making the client the most important person in the room.

I would therefore like to offer you a challenge as you read this book – or, if you have already read it, as you reflect upon it. Ask yourself: how often do I discuss these topics with my clients?

To illustrate this point, let us look at what has happened in the world of medicine, and what we might learn from the humble stethoscope.

THE STETHOSCOPE AND
THE DANGERS OF TECHNOLOGY

Many people who manage their own investments or create their own financial plans take great care over their processes. And rightly so – one incorrect assumption about growth or tax can have an enormous impact when compounded over 30 years.

Similarly, cashflow forecasting has been the predominant tool for financial planners over the past decade. Sometimes, however, a focus on the technology can distract from the important questions.

To illustrate this point, let us digress briefly to look at developments in medicine over the past two hundred years.[138]

THE INVENTION OF THE STETHOSCOPE

Back in the early 19th century, the only way that a doctor could find out what was happening inside a patient's body was to ask them. The patient's description of their symptoms provided the only clues that the doctor had to go on.

One physician changed all that.

In 1816, Dr René Laennec was examining a rather buxom female patient. In order to obtain additional information, he put his ear to her chest but, frustratingly, was unable to hear anything. He then took a piece of card, rolled it into a tube, and pressed one end to the lady's chest and his ear to the other.

To his amazement, he could now hear the beating of her heart and the rhythm of her breathing.

Inspired, Dr Laennec went to his workshop and built the world's first stethoscope – a wooden conical tube narrower at one end than the other. He then wrote an article in a medical journal expounding his new idea. He developed his invention, as did others, and the stethoscope as we know it today was born.

BYPASSING THE PATIENT

Up to this point, the only way that doctors could get information was by way of a conversation. Now, doctors were able to understand what was happening inside the patient's body without having to rely on the patient.

This started a key principle in modern medicine – the expertise of the doctor above that of the patient. It began a process that has developed over the ensuing two centuries. More tools have been developed, and now we have ultrasound, MRI scanners, X-rays and many other ways of seeing what is happening inside the patient's body.

Now doctors can tell you what is wrong with you without having to talk to you at all!

But has something been lost in the process?

MY LOCAL GP SERVICE

At my local GP surgery, there are several places to park a car. The first parking spaces are immediately next to the surgery itself. There is a car park a little behind the surgery. Finally, there is a shoppers' car park over the road.

There is a sign next to the parking spaces closest to the entrance that reads 'Doctors' Parking Only.'

Over the years, I have suffered from gout. When I visit the surgery, I must park in one of the two car parks further away, often walking with a serious limp and in pain, even sometimes only with the aid of crutches. I need to walk around the building, past the doctors' parking spaces, in order to enter the surgery.

As I am walking past the doctors' cars, I can't help but wonder – has the balance of the doctor–patient relationship shifted too far?

WHO IS THE MOST IMPORTANT PERSON IN THE ROOM?

Returning to diagnosis, the ability to look inside the body means that Western conventional medicine often dispenses with listening to the patient completely.

GPs in the UK now have an eight-minute slot in which to diagnose the patient's problem. Doctors interrupt their patients within 11 seconds on average, even though patients need at least 29 seconds just to describe their symptoms.[139]

If it is something serious, the patient might be sent off for some tests. This could result in a session with a consultant. Despite never having met the patient before, and without any discussion with the patient about their life, the consultant presents their diagnosis and their remedy.

Medical science has become excellent at telling us *what* is wrong with us. In the process, has it forgotten to ask *why*?

THE TROUBLE WITH
FINANCIAL TECHNOLOGY

Look around at all the ways in which your clients can access information about money. Online banking apps make it easier to check your balance. Payment through your phone. Managing investments through online platforms.

This is doubly so within the financial advice world. Think, for example, of the ability to complete attitude-to-risk questionnaires outside the meeting. Or client portals to update information directly, leaving the meeting free to discuss investment portfolios.

Most notable in this respect is the cashflow forecast, a fabulous tool that enables the adviser to project clients' financial position sforward to see what the future holds.

But is the cashflow the equivalent of the MRI scanner? It enables an adviser to diagnose the financial ills of a client without even talking to them.

When used well, cashflow forecasts can help the client to dream about future possibilities and then ground them in reality by forecasting scenarios. When used poorly, however, a cashflow forecast can have the opposite effect – projecting the current position and grounding the client to their existing assumptions and self-limiting beliefs.

Financial technology has developed in such a way that it can track, analyse and report on everything about your money except that which makes life worthwhile.[140]

> I once heard a marketing consultant, Lucien Camp, give a talk to advisers at a conference. He was talking about what fee levels advisers should charge, and the perception that more meetings are what clients want.
>
> "My adviser called me up," he explained. "He told me that he had good news and bad news. The bad news was that their charges were going to double, from 0.5% to 1% of assets per annum. The good news, however, was that the annual review was going to become a quarterly review. He asked if that would be ok.
>
> "I replied that he could put the charges up to 2% per annum if he wanted, as long as he promised to never come and see me again!"[142]

CONCLUSION

Surely one of the greatest quotes from a movie is this from *Jurassic Park* (1993): "Your scientists were so preoccupied with whether or not they could, they didn't stop to think if they should."

Technology has obviously changed the world for better in so many ways. It is important, however, not to lose sight of what is important – of the sources of happiness. Money should be an engine for joy. The same goes for technology.

NOTES

1. Chris Budd, *The Financial Wellbeing Book* (London: LID Publishing, 2016).

2. I was once taught, during a training session on making presentations, that the structure should always be "Tell 'em what you're going to tell 'em; tell 'em; then tell 'em what you've told them." This section fulfils the first part of that mantra!

3. This statistic is from my memory of the advert.

4. From chapter 64 of the *Dao De Jing*.

5. From slogan 1 of *Lojong*. See "The 59 Slogans of Lojong" (The Buddhaful Tao), last modified 4 July 2012, https://thebuddhafultao.wordpress.com/tag/lojong.

6. Gelong Thubten, *A Monk's Guide to Happiness* (London: Yellow Kite, 2019).

7. *Our Insight to the Nation's Financial Wellbeing 2022* (Aegon, 2022), accessed 7 March 2023, https://www.aegon.co.uk/content/dam/ukpaw/documents/financial-wellbeing-index-summary.pdf.

8. "Cultivating a Good Heart" (Dalai Lama), last modified 10 November 2021, https://www.dalailama.com/news/2021/cultivating-a-good-heart.

9. These examples are all taken from Rutger Bregman, *Humankind: A Hopeful History* (London: Bloomsbury, 2020).

10. Mark McCormack, *What They Don't Teach You at Harvard Business School* (London: HarperCollins, 1994).

11. At least I *think* it was Richard Gere who said that. As Mark Twain once said, "Nobody minds being incorrectly attributed to a quote as long as it is a good one."

12. Quoted in Susan Ratcliffe, ed., *Oxford Essential Quotations* (Oxford University Press, 2016), accessed 7 March 2023, https://www.oxfordreference.com.

13. To paraphrase Carl Richards of Behavior Gap in episode 15 of *The Financial Wellbeing Podcast* (see https://www.financialwell-being.co.uk/podcasts).

14. As outlined in the book *Thinking Fast and Slow* by Daniel Kahneman (London: Penguin, 2011).

15. Taken from Rutger Bregman, *Utopia for Realists: And How We Can Get There* (London: Bloomsbury, 2017).

16. World Bank (Data.worldbank.org).

17. "Early Occupational Pension Schemes" (The Pensions Archive), accessed 23 March 2023, https://www.pensionsarchive.org.uk/77.

18. Sarah Laskow, "How Retirement Was Invented" (*The Atlantic*), last modified 24 October 2014, https://www.theatlantic.com/business/archive/2014/10/how-retirement-was-invented/381802.

19. From a debate in the House of Commons on 29 June 1908. See "Old-Age Pensions Bill" (Hansard), accessed 7 March 2023, https://api.parliament.uk/historic-hansard/commons/1908/jun/29/old-age-pensions-bill.

20. This quote actually goes back to ancient times but was, of course, popularised by that fount of aphorisms, Spiderman.

21. This phrase was used by behavioural finance expert Greg Davies in episode 25 of *The Financial Wellbeing Podcast* (see https://www.financialwell-being.co.uk/podcasts).

22. This true story was told to me by an oncology staff nurse.

23. "Funds Hit by £7.6bn Outflows, as Economic Uncertainty Intensifies Following 'Mini Budget'" (The Investment Association), last modified 3 November 2022, https://www.theia.org/media/press-releases/funds-hit-ps76bn-outflows-economic-uncertainty-intensifies-following-mini.

24. For a meta-analysis of the research, see Pengmin Qin and Georg Northoff, "How Is Our Self Related to Midline Regions and the Default-Mode Network?" *NeuroImage* 57, no. 3 (2011): 1221–33.

25. Jordi Quoidbach, Daniel T. Gilbert and Timothy D. Wilson, "The End of History Illusion" (*Science*), last modified 4 January 2023, https://www.science.org/doi/10.1126/science.1229294.

26. Hal E. Hershfield, Daniel G. Goldstein, William F. Sharpe, Jesse Fox, Leo Yeykelis, Laura L. Carstensen and Jeremy N. Bailenson, "Increasing Saving Behavior through Age-Progressed Renderings of the Future Self," *Journal of Marketing Research* 48 (2011): S23–37.

27. "New Study: Financial Wellbeing Is More about Mindset than Money" (Aegon), last modified 29 March 2021, https://www.aegon.com/newsroom/news/2021/aegon-financial-wellbeing-index-2021.

28. See https://bslm.org.uk.

29. Rangan Chatterjee, *The Stress Solution* (London: Penguin, 2018).

30. Let's go with a study from the psychology department of Carnegie Mellon University Sheldon Cohen and Sarah D. Pressman, "Positive Affect and Health," *Current Directions in Psychological Science* 15, no. 3 (2006): 122–25.

31. Ingrid Torjesen, "Social Prescribing Could Help Alleviate Pressure on GPs," *The BMJ* 352 (2016): i1436.

32. *A Very General Practice* (Citizens Advice, 2015), accessed 7 March 2023, https://www.citizensadvice.org.uk/Global/CitizensAdvice/Public%20services%20publications/CitizensAdvice_AVeryGeneralPractice_May2015.pdf.

33. Robert Waldinger, "What Makes a Good Life? Lessons from the Longest Study on Happiness" (TED), last modified 25 January 2016, https://www.youtube.com/watch?v=8KkKuTCFvzl.

34. Mike Dixon, *Time to Heal* (London: Unicorn, 2020); Rangan Chatterjee, *The Stress Solution* (London: Penguin, 2018).

35. Rangan Chatterjee, *The Stress Solution* (London: Penguin, 2018).

36. Ed Diener and Robert Biswas-Diener, *Happiness: Unlocking the Mysteries of Psychological Wealth* (Malden, MA: Blackwell, 2008).

37. See Larry Gonick and Tim Kasser, *Hypercapitalism* (New York: New Press, 2018).

38. Nelson Mandela, *Long Walk to Freedom* (London: Abacus, 1994).

39. This section is inspired and informed by *Humankind: A Hopeful History* by Rutger Bregman (London: Bloomsbury, 2020), a book that gives a thorough explanation of why we are fundamentally good.

40. This is brilliantly outlined and expanded on in *Humankind*.

41. This is a very Buddhist principle, part of the teaching known as 'dependent arising.'

42. The 'Nature and Nurture' chapter of *Happiness* delves deeply into the research on this subject. See Ed Diener and Robert Biswas-Diener, *Happiness: Unlocking the Mysteries of Psychological Wealth* (Malden, MA: Blackwell, 2008).

43. The theory is summarised in various sources, including Sonja Lyubomirsky, *The How of Happiness* (London: Sphere, 2007).

44. The percentages in this section are taken from Sonja Lyubomirsky, *The How of Happiness* (London: Sphere, 2007).

45. As the Harvard study on Happiness did, as explained in the TED Talk on this subject by Robert Waldinger – a video that, at time of writing, has been seen over 43 million times! See Robert Waldinger, "What Makes a Good Life? Lessons from the Longest Study on Happiness" (TED), last modified 23 December 2015, https://www.ted.com/talks/robert_waldinger_what_makes_a_good_life_lessons_from_the_longest_study_on_happiness/no-comments.

46. A phrase taken from Sonja Lyubomirsky's *The How of Happiness* (London: Sphere, 2007).

47. Gelong Thubten, *A Monk's Guide to Happiness* (London: Yellow Kite, 2019); Martin Stepek, *A Pocket Guide to a Mindful Life* (n.p.: Cadzow-Haczow Books, 2018).

48. Shalom H. Schwartz, "An Overview of the Schwartz Theory of Basic Values," *Online Readings in Psychology and Culture* 2, no. 1 (2012), https://scholarworks.gvsu.edu/orpc/vol2/iss1/11.

49. In addition to the book *Hypercapitalism* (New York: New Press, 2018), see the interview Professor Kasser gave to *The Financial Wellbeing Podcast* in episodes 42 and 46 (see https://www.financialwell-being.co.uk/podcasts).

50. Self-determination theory has been around for many decades. It was accepted in psychology circles in the mid-1980s following the publication of Edward L. Deci and Richard Ryan's *Self-Determination and Intrinsic Motivation in Human Behaviour* (New York: Plenum Press, 1985).

51. Robert Waldinger, "What Makes a Good Life? Lessons from the Longest Study on Happiness" (TED), last modified 25 January 2016, https://www.youtube.com/watch?v=8KkKuTCFvzl.

52. See Daniel Pink, *Drive: The Surprising Truth about What Motivates Us* (New York: Penguin, 2009).

53. Yannick Stephan, Evelyne Fouquereau and Anne Fernandez, "The Relation between Self-Determination and Retirement Satisfaction among Active Retired Individuals," *International Journal of Aging and Human Development* 66, no. 4 (2008): 329–45.

54. Andrew Steptoe, Angus Deaton and Arthur A. Stone, "Subjective Wellbeing, Health, and Ageing," *The Lancet* 385, no. 9968: 640–48.

55. Amy Patterson Neubert, "Money Only Buys Happiness for a Certain Amount" (Purdue University), last modified 13 February 2018, https://www.purdue.edu/newsroom/releases/2018/Q1/money-only-buys-happiness-for-a-certain-amount.html.

56. Tom Rath and Jim Harter, *Wellbeing* (New York: Gallup, 2010).

57. I listed these five elements in *The Financial Wellbeing Book* (London: LID Publishing, 2016) and here I go into them in a little more detail.

58. Robert Waldinger, "What Makes a Good Life? Lessons from the Longest Study on Happiness" (TED), last modified 25 January 2016, https://www.youtube.com/watch?v=8KkKuTCFvzl.

59. Chris Budd, *The Financial Wellbeing Book* (London: LID Publishing, 2016); *Financial Well-Being: The Goal of Financial Education* (Consumer Financial Protection Bureau, 2015), accessed 22 March 2023, https://files.consumerfinance.gov/f/201501_cfpb_report_financial-well-being.pdf.

60. *The Art of Happiness: A Handbook for Living* by the Dalai Lama and Howard C. Cutler (London: Hodder and Stoughton, 1998) is especially informative on this point.

61. This idea also features in the title of an excellent book by money coach Mark Bristow, *The Financial Healer: Change Your Self-Worth, Increase Your Net Worth* (Bramham: Zento Publishing, 2015).

62. "New Study: Financial Wellbeing Is More about Mindset than Money" (Aegon), last modified 29 March 2021, https://www.aegon.com/newsroom/news/2021/aegon-financial-wellbeing-index-2021.

63. Self-determination theory is a very broad topic; I am only scratching the surface in this book. As mentioned, the original book on the subject is Edward L. Deci and Richard Ryan's *Self-Determination and Intrinsic Motivation in Human Behaviour* (New York: Plenum Press, 1985), which is extremely thorough!

64. From a study conducted by Neil during his time with Be-IQ (the behavioural insight company he founded in 2013) and shared with me.

65. See *Drive* by Daniel Pink (New York: Penguin, 2009) for more on this topic.

66. Susan Scutti, "Michael Phelps: 'I am extremely thankful that I did not take my life,'" last modified 20 January 2018, https://edition.cnn.com/2018/01/19/health/michael-phelps-depression/index.html.

67. "Performance Decompression: Post-games Celebration and Support" (English Institute of Sport, 2021), accessed 23 March 2023, https://eis2win.co.uk/article/performance-decompression-post-games-celebration-and-support.

68. Quoted in Jack Guy, "New York Billionaire Michael Steinhardt Surrenders $70 Million of Stolen Ancient Art," last modified 7 December 2021, https://edition.cnn.com/style/article/michael-steinhardt-ancient-art-surrender-scli-intl/index.html.

69. This is a true story, but I have changed the name of the firm.

70. The Institute for Financial Wellbeing offers coaching courses (https://instituteforfinancialwellbeing.com).

71. Paul Dolan, *Happiness by Design* (London: Penguin, 2015).

72. Vishvapani Blomfield, *Guatama Buddha: The Life and Teachings of the Awakened One* (London: Quercus, 2011).

73. Neil Gaiman, "Inspirational Commencement Speech at the University of the Arts 2012" (YouTube), last modified 23 May 2012, https://www.youtube.com/watch?v=ikAb-NYksel.

74. This is a core Buddhist precept – part of the Three Marks of Existence – called 'conditionality,' which refers to creating the conditions in your life that will allow you to thrive.

75. Jeff Tweedy, *How to Write One Song* (London: Faber & Faber, 2020).

76. Cutler uses the term 'pleasure' to describe what I am calling 'happiness,' and 'happiness' to describe what I am calling 'wellbeing.' I've changed these terms to keep the language consistent in this book. See *The Art of Happiness: A Handbook for Living* by the Dalai Lama and Howard C. Cutler (London: Hodder and Stoughton, 1998).

77. More coaching questions that advisers might use can be found in the book *Great Coaching Questions* by Nick Howell (n.p.: FCM Publishing, 2021).

78. My *The Financial Wellbeing Book* (London: LID Publishing, 2016) can help with this if you can't afford or don't want to engage a financial planner.

79. Research by Sheldon Cohen of Carnegie Mellon University, as reported in Richard J. Davidson and Sharon Begley, *The Emotional Life of Your Brain* (London: Hodder, 2012).

80. Richard J. Davidson and Sharon Begley, *The Emotional Life of Your Brain* (London: Hodder, 2012).

81. Richard J. Davidson and Sharon Begley, *The Emotional Life of Your Brain* (London: Hodder, 2012).

82. With specific thanks to Neil Bage for this insight.

83. A quote attributed to various authors but with no clear source.

84. J. P. Gerber, Ladd Wheeler and Jerry Suls, "A Social Comparison Theory Meta-analysis 60+ Years On," *Psychological Bulletin* 144, no. 2 (2018): 177–97.

85. Abraham H. Maslow, "A Theory of Human Motivation," *Psychological Review* 50, no. 4 (1943): 370–96.

86. Sonja Lyubomirsky, *The How of Happiness* (London: Piatkus, 2010).

87. As cited by Oliver Burkeman in his book *The Antidote* (Edinburgh: Canongate, 2013).

88. A template for a financial wellbeing report is available for those who complete the Financial Wellbeing Certificate from the Institute for Financial Wellbeing.

89. The Dalai Lama and Desmond Tutu, *The Book of Joy* (New York: Avery, 2016).

90. A phrase borrowed from the excellent book *Giving Is Good for You* by John Nickson (London: Biteback, 2013).

91. In a conversation with the Chief Executive of Philanthropy Impact.

92. You can read the full version at Kim Bendall, "The Butterfly Effect" (Institute for Financial Wellbeing), last modified 14 October 2020, https://instituteforfinancialwellbeing.com/the-butterfly-effect-by-kim-bendall.

93. As defined in the *Oxford English Dictionary*.

94. Philanthropy training courses are available through the Institute for Financial Wellbeing.

95. For more on this topic, see Elizabeth Dunn and Michael I. Norton, *Happy Money: The New Science of Smarter Spending* (London: Oneworld, 2014).

96. Jeroen Nawijn, Miquelle A. Marchand, Ruut Veenhoven and Ad J. Vingerhoets, "Vacationers Happier, but Most Not Happier After a Holiday," *Applied Research in Quality of Life* 5, no. 1 (2010): 35–47.

97. Recounted in Elizabeth Dunn and Michael I. Norton, *Happy Money: The New Science of Smarter Spending* (London: Oneworld, 2014).

98. Recounted in Elizabeth Dunn and Michael I. Norton, *Happy Money: The New Science of Smarter Spending* (London: Oneworld, 2014).

99. A big thank-you to my friend Neil Bage is needed here. Neil and I have worked together on a number of projects, and spoken at many events together, and much of my understanding of behavioural finance comes from him.

100. Two good books on this subject are Morgan Housel's *The Psychology of Money* (Petersfield: Harriman House, 2022) and Brian Portnoy's *The Geometry of Wealth* (Petersfield: Harriman House, 2018).

101. Justin Kruger and David Dunning, "Unskilled and Unaware of It: How Difficulties in Recognising One's Own Incompetence Lead to Inflated Self-Assessments," *Journal of Personality and Social Psychology* 77, no. 6 (1999): 1121–34.

102. This itself is a version of a quote from the English poet and satirist Alexander Pope. There really is very little that is truly new!

103. There is an interesting age factor to investing. Research from Aegon UK showed that 15% of 16- to 24-year-olds sold some or all of their investments when the stock market took a sudden dip, compared to only 2% of people aged over 55. See "New Study: Financial Wellbeing Is More about Mindset than Money" (Aegon), last modified 29 March 2021, https://www.aegon.com/newsroom/news/2021/aegon-financial-wellbeing-index-2021.

104. See Stanford marshmallow experiment – Wikipedia.

105. Episode 25 of *The Financial Wellbeing Podcast* (see https://www.financialwell-being.co.uk/podcasts).

106. There are many articles on this topic. See, for example, Carey K. Morewedge Lisa L. Shu, Daniel T. Gilbert and Timothy D. Wilson, "Bad Riddance or Good Rubbish? Ownership and Not Loss Aversion Causes the Endowment Effect," *Journal of Experimental Social Psychology* 45, no. 4 (2009): 947–51.

107. Sonja Lyubomirsky, *The How of Happiness* (London: Piatkus, 2010).

108. One model for this is David A. Kolb's Cycle of Learning, as outlined in *The Financial Wellbeing Book* (London: LID Publishing, 2016).

109. Matt Roper, *101 Crazy Ways To Die* (London: Michael Joseph, 2008).

110. This is the concept of 'impermanence' in Buddhism, and it is also an element of Hinduism. Everything, whether physical or mental, is changing all the time; desire and attachment are therefore likely to lead to suffering.

111. The Dalai Lama and Desmond Tutu, *The Book of Joy* (New York: Avery, 2016).

112. This is also the message taught by the Stoics. They used to teach that nothing outside your own mind can truly be said to be positive or negative. The only things that cause suffering are the beliefs that we hold.

113. My thanks to licensed clinical psychologist and co-founder of Shaping Wealth Dr Joy Lere for contributing to this section on permission.

114. The documentary *Ben Stokes: Phoenix from the Ashes* (2022) is fascinating on the benefits of allowing yourself to fail.

115. I am especially indebted to Dr Lere for this idea.

116. *See* David Finch, "The Power of Permission" (*Psychology Today*), last modified 9 December 2013, https://www.psychologytoday.com/gb/blog/the-journal-best-practices/201312/the-power-permission.

117. Taylor Lorenz, "Young Creators Are Burning Out and Breaking Down" (*New York Times*), last modified 17 September 2021, https://www.nytimes.com/2021/06/08/style/creator-burnout-social-media.html.

118. Episode 83, *The Financial Wellbeing Podcast* (see https://www.financialwell-being.co.uk/podcasts).

119. See episode 32 of *The Financial Wellbeing Podcast* (https://www.financialwell-being.co.uk/podcasts) and Maria Nedeva's book *Never Bet On Red: How to Pay Off Debt and Live Debt Free* (n.p.: Scott Dixon, 2020).

120. Karen J. Pine and Simonne Gnessen's book *Sheconomics* (London: Headline, 2009) is excellent on the detail of getting control of your personal finances.

121. Molly Liebergall, "Author Talks: The World's Longest Study of Adult Development Finds the Key to Happy Living" (McKinsey & Company), last modified 16 February 2023, https://www.mckinsey.com/featured-insights/mckinsey-on-books/author-talks-the-worlds-longest-study-of-adult-development-finds-the-key-to-happy-living.

122. See https://instituteforfinancialwellbeing.com/learning-development.

123. My thanks to Jan Bowen-Nielsen of Quiver Management for sense-checking these exercises for me.

124. With thanks to Sarah Newcomb of Morningstar, and acknowledging the work of Hal Hershfield, upon which these ideas are based. For more on this, see *Your Future Self* by Hal Hershfield.

125. Thanks for this idea to Dr Thomas Mathar of Aegon, who has been conducting research into role models and our future self.

126. "New Study: Financial Wellbeing Is More about Mindset than Money" (Aegon), last modified 29 March 2021, https://www.aegon.com/newsroom/news/2021/aegon-financial-wellbeing-index-2021.

127. From a search of the market (assuming the individuals were non-smokers) by Ovation Finance Ltd in September 2022.

128. This is a summary of a much more detailed exercise described in *The Financial Wellbeing Book* (London: LID Publishing, 2016).

129. The website https://www.charitychoice.co.uk/charities lists all charities by sector.

130. You might find a relevant website – in Bristol, for example, there is the website https://www.bristolcharities.org.uk. For larger donations, consider your local community foundation.

131. The principle of this exercise is based on a more detailed exercise used by Simonne Gnessen of Wise Monkey Coaching and is used here with her permission.

132. Thanks to Dr Joy Lere of Shaping Wealth for this exercise.

133. See the Harvard Health Publishing website (search https://www.health.harvard.edu/search for the names of the four chemicals), although there are many, many sources of information on these four chemicals.

134. Carl J. Charnetski and Francis X. Brennan, "Sexual Frequency and Salivary Immunoglobulin A (IgA)," *Psychological Reports* 94, no. 3 (2004): 839–44.

135. Simon Young, "How to Increase Serotonin in the Human Brain without Drugs," *Journal of Psychiatry and Neuroscience* 32, no. 6 (2007): 394–99.

136. The Role of Oxytocin in the Dog–Owner Relationship by Marshall-Pescini, et al. https://www.ncbi.nlm.nih.gov/pmc/articles/PMC6826447/.

137. As said to me by Dr Joy Lere of Shaping Wealth.

138. This section was inspired by episode 270 of the podcast *99% Invisible* (https://99percentinvisible.org).

139. Stephen Trzeciak and Anthony Mazzarelli, *Compassionomics: The Revolutionary Scientific Evidence that Caring Makes a Difference* (Pensacola: Studer Group, 2019).

140. To paraphrase Bobby Kennedy's famous speech at the University of Kansas in 1968.

141. Lucien Camp, in a talk delivered at the Institute of Financial Planning conference, Wales, 2015.

AUTHOR'S NOTES AND THANKS

The objective of this book is to bring together lots of research and ideas from many different walks of life into one cohesive treatise on the relationship between money and happiness.

In bringing together these ideas around financial planning, I have sought existing content from many different areas. Nothing wrong in borrowing other people's ideas as long as you give them due credit, which I hope I have done.

Some of these ideas are easily connected with a book about financial planning. The link with others might previously have been a bit less obvious. And the sources of some are often best not mentioned at all – using the word 'Buddhism' in a room full of financial advisers does not always get the positive reaction one might be seeking!

In particular, this book would not have been possible without the generosity and wisdom of Neil Bage of Shaping Wealth. He is an expert in human behaviour and is one of the kindest and most giving people I know. I've no idea how that combination of characteristics could exist in one person, but if anyone could explain it to me, it would be Neil.

Others without whom I would not have been able to write this book include:
Tom Morris and Adrian Kidd of Ovation Finance Ltd
Jan Bowen-Nielsen
Dr Thomas Mathar of Aegon

The team at the Institute for Financial Wellbeing (IFW)

The IFW stemmed from an idle tweet one bored Thursday afternoon in January 2019. That led to me holding a financial wellbeing conference, which led to the founding of the institute. There are many people who have put time into getting the IFW off the ground. My particular thanks to:

Nick Marsh, CEO, who has put so much effort into establishing the organisation. Also the current board, who give their time for free: Tom Morris, Lorraine McFall, Rebecca Tuck, Ruth Sturkey, Harjeet Heer and Charles Goodman.

Andy Manson of Aegon, whose support for the IFW from the outset has been instrumental in enabling the institute to become established.

Sarah Lyon of Parmenion, who believed in this topic right from that very first conference.

And for support and giving of time: Simonne Gnessen, Catherine Morgan, Erik Porter, Emily Pool, Hiren Panchal, Ian Dowe, Dennis Harhalakis, Mymy Nguyen, Funmi Olufunwa, Helena Wardle and Adam Owen.

FURTHER READING

Many of the insights in this book were taken from, or inspired by, interviews and research undertaken for the writing of *The Financial Wellbeing Podcast* since its beginning in 2016. My thanks to my co-hosts of that podcast, Tom 'Tommo' Morris and David Lloyd.

What follow are other books that I would recommend if you're interested in studying this area further. Standing above them all, for me, is *The Book of Joy* by the Dalai Lama and Archbishop Desmond Tutu with Douglas Abrams (New York: Avery, 2016), a genuine life changer in the way I looked at the world. It is a book that can be read many times, the sort of book you find yourself buying multiple copies of, then handing out to friends with a knowing smile.

ON WELLBEING IN GENERAL

Bregman, Rutger. *Humankind: A Hopeful History*. London: Bloomsbury, 2020.

Burkeman, Oliver. *The Antidote*. London: Vintage, 2018.

Chatterjee, Rangan. *The Stress Solution*. London: Penguin, 2018.

Clark, Fleche, et al. *The Origins of Happiness*. New Jersey: Princeton University Press, 2018.

Dalai Lama and Howard C. Cutler. *The Art of Happiness: A Handbook for Living*. London: Hodder and Stoughton, 1998.

Davidson, Richard J., and Sharon Begley. *The Emotional Life of Your Brain*. London: Hodder, 2012.

Diener, Ed, and Robert Biswas-Diener. *Happiness: Unlocking the Mysteries of Psychological Wealth*. Malden, MA: Blackwell, 2008.

Dolan, Paul. *Happiness by Design*. London: Penguin, 2015.

King, Vanessa. *10 Keys To Happier Living*. London: Headline, 2016.

Layard, Richard. *Can We Be Happier?* London: Pelican, 2020.

Lyubomirsky, Sonja. *The How of Happiness*. London: Piatkus, 2010.

Lyubomirsky, Sonja. *The Myths of Happiness*. London: Penguin, 2014.

Pink, Daniel. *Drive: The Surprising Truth about What Motivates Us*. New York: Penguin, 2009.

Rath, Tom, and Jim Harter. *Wellbeing*. New York: Gallup, 2010.

Stepek, Martin. *A Pocket Guide to a Mindful Life*. n.p.: Cadzow-Haczow Books, 2018.

Thubten, Gelong. *A Monk's Guide to Happiness*. London: Yellow Kite, 2019.

Tweedy, Jeff. *How to Write One Song*. London: Faber & Faber, 2020.

Waldinger, Robert., and Schultz, Mark. *The Good Life*. London: Ebury, 2023.

ON MONEY AND HAPPINESS

Bristow, Mark. *The Financial Healer: Change Your Self-Worth, Increase Your Net Worth*. Bramham: Zento Publishing, 2015.

Budd, Chris. *The Financial Wellbeing Book*. London: LID Publishing, 2016.

Dunn, Elizabeth, and Michael I. Norton. *Happy Money: The New Science of Smarter Spending*. London: Oneworld, 2014.

Gonick, Larry, and Tim Kasser. *Hypercapitalism*. New York: New Press, 2018.

Matthew, Pete. *The Meaningful Money Handbook*. Petersfield: Harriman House, 2018.

Nickson, John. *Giving Is Good for You*. London: Biteback, 2013.

Pine, Karen J., and Simonne Gnessen. *Sheconomics*. London: Headline, 2009.

Portnoy, Brian. *The Geometry of Wealth*. Petersfield: Harriman House, 2018.

FOR FINANCIAL ADVISERS AND FINANCIAL PLANNERS

Howell, Nick. *Great Coaching Questions*. Lincoln: FCM Publishing, 2021.

Kline, Nancy. *Time To Think*. London: Cassell, 2002.

Rosenberg, Marshall B. *Nonviolent Communication*. California: Puddle Dancer Press, 2015.

Scarlett, David. *The Soul Millionaire*. Springtime Books, 2011.

Summers, Moira. *Advice That Sticks*. Practical Inspiration Publishing, 2020.

ABOUT THE AUTHOR

Chris Budd founded financial planning company Ovation Finance Ltd in 2000. He sold a majority of Ovation to an Employee Ownership Trust (EOT) in March 2018.

He is the author of six books, including the original book about financial wellbeing which he wrote in 2015, *The Financial Wellbeing Book*. He wrote *The Eternal Business* to provide a guide for owners to the EOT transition process. He has also published three novels with a fourth in progress.

Chris has been writing and presenting The Financial Wellbeing Podcast since 2016. He founded the Institute for Financial Wellbeing (IFW) to bring together financial advisers and planners who want to focus on their clients' happiness, not just their money.

Chris lives in Somerset with his family and too many guitars.